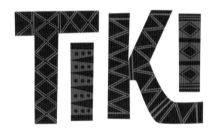

# PALM SPRINGS TIKI!

## Polynesia in the Desert

SVEN KIRSTEN • PETER MORUZZI

Gibbs Smith

FIRST EDITION
28 27 26 25 24     5 4 3 2 1

Published by

Gibbs Smith

570 N. Sportsplex Dr.

Kaysville, UT 84037


1.800.835.4993 orders

www.gibbs-smith.com


Design by Ryan Thomann and Sven Kirsten

Printed and bound in China


Library of Congress Control Number: 2023952694

ISBN: 978-1-4236-6603-5


This product is made of FSC®-certified and other controlled material.

FSC
www.fsc.org

MIX
Paper | Supporting
responsible forestry
FSC® C153458

# Contents

Acknowledgments | 7

Introduction | 9

1 ✦ Early Escapist Concepts in Southern California & Palm Springs | 11

2 ✦ Other Worlds to Explore | 29

3 ✦ Polynesia in the Desert | 43

4 ✦ The Chi Chi Nightclubs | 61

5 ✦ The Look of Tiki: Waltah Clarke | 73

6 ✦ Clif and Lou Sawyer—Premiere Purveyors of Polynesian Pop | 85

7 ✦ Don the Beachcomber—a Palm Springs Institution | 99

8 ✦ Idols and A-Frames | 113

9 ✦ Tiki Motor Hotels in the Desert | 131

10 ✦ Aloha Jhoe's—A Tiki Gesamtkunstwerk | 147

11 ✦ Deep Desert Tiki | 161

12 ✦ Palm Springs Tiki Today | 181

Conclusion | 195

Photo Credits | 197

About the Authors | 198

# ACKNOWLEDGMENTS

The authors wish to thank the collectors, artists, photographers, authors, and historians who have contributed their talents to making this book a feast for the eyes:

| | | |
|---|---|---|
| Josh Agle | Kiara Geller | Dug Miller |
| Linda Beal | Valerie Gerdes | Angelica Navarro |
| Amy Boylan | Mike Gilbert | Charles Phoenix |
| Sammy Brookes | Tim Glazner | Jordan Reichek |
| Renee Brown | Donald Haas | Scott Schell |
| Daniel M. Callahan | Donald Harvey | Al Scott |
| Anthony Carpenter | Jochen Hirschfeld | Rory Snyder |
| Brian Chidester | Randy Jensen | Otto von Stroheim |
| Tracy Conrad | Frank Jones | Tiki Tom-Tom |
| Becky Ebenkamp | Donna Burns Kennedy | Kurt Wahlner |
| Bruce Emerton | Martin Lindsay | |
| Ron Ferrell | Tayva Martinez | |

# INTRODUCTION

The concept of creating South Sea islands in the desert is deliciously rife with absurdity. As such, it deserves to be explored beyond the "opposites attract" adage one could apply to a phenomenon where modernism and primitivism spectacularly coincided.

Hawaii and Palm Springs both became popular vacation spots in twentieth-century America. They shared the elements of palms and pools and sun and sand that said, "I'm on vacation!" Both served as glamorous getaways for celebrities and business moguls, inspiring a newly affluent middle class to follow in their footsteps.

Famous bandleader Horace Heidt understood the affinity between the two destinations. After opening the Lone Palm Hotel in Palm Springs in 1946, he launched a new apartment complex in California's San Fernando Valley eponymously named Horace Heidt Estates. He christened the two separate sections of the property Hawaiian Village and Palm Springs, symbolically bringing together island and desert flair in one locale.

Tikis guard the entrance to Horace Heidt Estates in Sherman Oaks where Hawaii and Palm Springs are two sides of the same coin.

The *Walled Oasis of Biskra*, as it will rise amid palms, overlooking the *Coachella Valley*.

*Sketched by Mark Daniels.*

**ABOVE:** The "Walled Oasis of Biskra" was one of the earliest flights of fancy by developers in the Palm Springs area.

**OPPOSITE:** Mural of the famed Queen Califia, name giver to California, by Maynard Dixon, 1926.

# 1

# EARLY ESCAPIST CONCEPTS
## in Southern California & Palm Springs

**W**hat's in a name? In the case of California, it was a romance writer's fantasy describing a mythical island inhabited by tall black warrior women:

"Know this, due East of the Indies is an island called California, just by the terrestrial paradise, populated by black amazons. . . . They were clad in armors of gold, as were the beasts they rode. . . . There reigned in the island of California the mighty and beautiful Queen Califia . . . " –Garci Ordóñez Rodríguez de Montalvo

With its name based on fiction, California was predestined to become the home of utopian concepts and fanciful appellations.

When sunseekers and trailblazers from the East Coast and middle-American states migrated to the promised land of Califia to stake their claim, they too chose names from legends for their new lands. Mythical places like Avalon and Arcadia were invoked, as well as faraway romantic locales like Venice and the legendary Alhambra castle. Fictitious adventure heroes like Tarzan became Tarzana.

**TOP:** The name for Catalina Island's main village Avalon was taken from Arthurian lore.

**CENTER:** The suburban city of Alhambra adopted its moniker from a famous 13th-century Moorish castle in Spain.

**BOTTOM:** The real Alhambra in Granada, Spain.

AVALON, CATALINA ISLAND. LOOKING NORTH    J-63

California's Suburban
HOME PLACE
CITY of ALHAMBRA

THIRTY MINUTES
FROM BROADWAY
LOS ANGELES, CAL.

THIS BOOK IS OF VALUE TO THOSE INTERESTED
PLEASE DO NOT DESTROY
PASS IT ALONG

In Southern California, the warm Mediterranean climate inspired the area's motto "Land of Sunshine" and place names like Edendale and Tropico. Health apostles, evangelists, and spiritual seekers found sanctuary in communities like Krotona in the Hollywood hills and the "Semi-Tropical Spiritual Tract" in Echo Park near downtown Los Angeles.

The abundant sunshine and natural environs also attracted the young film industry looking for variety in locations and dependable good weather. With them, the movie companies brought performers, artists, and writers whose creative output established a new mythical locale: Hollywood

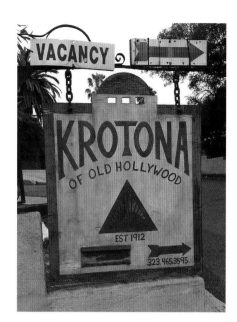
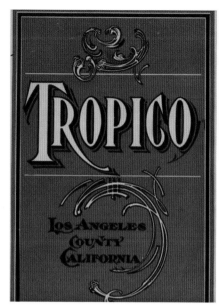

**TOP LEFT:** Krotona was a community founded in 1912 for the members of the Theosophical Society. Its name hailed from Kroton in ancient Greece, home of the school of philosopher Pythagoras.

**TOP RIGHT:** 1903 guide to the city of Tropico, now part of Glendale.

**RIGHT:** The name Arcadia, an idyllic haven in Greek and Renaissance mythology, was chosen for another LA suburb.

And then there were those sunseekers who wanted to get away from it all. Decrying the effects of industrialization and urbanism on the human condition, they espoused a back-to-nature lifestyle of vegetarianism, open air exercise, barefoot walking, and sunbathing.

The Lebensreform movement in Germany blossomed in the mid-nineteenth century, promoting spiritual and physical "renewal of life" through theosophy, yoga, naturopathy, and nudism. Writers and artists published books and magazines, and followers founded alternative communities.

William Pester was a Lebensreform believer who emigrated to America and chose the California desert as his place of refuge. He staked his claim in Tahquitz Canyon where he intended to "study himself with untrammeled nature as his classroom."

**TOP LEFT:** Palm trees and springs formed an oasis in the desert.

**BOTTOM LEFT:** "Light Prayer" depicts the essence of the Lebensreform movement.

**ABOVE:** William Pester partaking of the offerings of nature in Palm Springs, 1920.

Pester built himself a shack from palm wood and palm fronts—much like Robinson Crusoe, except in the desert, not on a desert island. There he foraged for plant food, collected rocks and Indian artifacts from the desert floor, and played his slide guitar. Once he became known as the "Hermit of Palm Springs," his chosen exile from civilization did not last. When the *Los Angeles Times* published a photo of him at his hermit's hut, the status of Palm Springs as a burgeoning tourist town brought the curious to his doorstep, then just a Model T ride away from town.

Pester made the best of it by selling walking sticks he fashioned from manzanita and other bushes, and after being the subject of many tourist "selfies," he had his own postcards made with Lebensreform wisdoms on the back. When he fled public life to the nearby city of Indio he chose to live under a water tank, his hut becoming an Indian trading post known as Hermit's Bench.

**TOP LEFT:** William Pester in front of his rustic hut, early 1920s.

**ABOVE TOP:** Robinson Crusoe in his self-built home.

**ABOVE:** Hollywood matinee idol Rudolph Valentino posing with Pester, 1924.

**ABOVE:** The California Nature Boys, a vanguard of 1960s counterculture. Eden Ahbez is on the lower left.

**RIGHT:** *Eden's Island*—The album that bridged Tiki and New Age culture.

NATURE BOY
by eden ahbez
As Recorded by NAT "KING" COLE - Capitol Record No. 15054

BURKE & VAN HEUSEN, INC.
MUSIC PUBLISHERS
By Arrangement with
CRESTVIEW MUSIC CORP.

The next dropout from civilization to follow in William Pester's footsteps was Eden Ahbez. Pester was long gone, but it seems likely that Ahbez knew of him. It is uncertain if that was sufficient inspiration for Ahbez to pen the hit song "Nature Boy." In conjuring its enchanting title character, the ballad possessed a strange hypnotic spell and simple beauty that distilled life to a single purpose. After having been recorded by Nat King Cole, the overwhelming success of Ahbez's composition cast him in the limelight and allowed him to record *Eden's Island*, the missing link between the Sinatra generation and the hippie youth movement.

Eden Ahbez joined a group of like-minded men called the Nature Boys who spent the winter months in the hills and caves above Palm Springs. With two of them he formed the Nature Boy Trio, playing in cafes in Palm Springs and beatnik clubs in Los Angeles.

**TOP CENTER:** The Eden Ahbez composition "Palm Springs" was recorded in 1959 by Ray Anthony for his *More Dream Dancing* album.

**TOP RIGHT:** Sheet music for the song that sold a million records and was covered by a generation of singers.

**BOTTOM RIGHT:** The only known photo of the Nature Boy Trio.

**ABOVE:** Fritzi Ridgeway's Pueblo Revival Hotel Del Tahquitz, 1928.

**OPPOSITE:** Cabot Yerxa surveying his handiwork.

## Escapist Architecture in the Desert

In the early twentieth century, exotic revival architecture flourished in America with architects taking cues from Egyptian, Moorish, and Mayan motifs. Pueblo Revival style became popular in New Mexico, inspired by the ancient Taos Pueblo. Hollywood actress Fritzi Ridgeway, known as the "cowgirl star," built Hotel Del Tahquitz, the first and only hotel in that style in Palm Springs. But the pueblo look did not catch on until the Southwest fad decades later.

This did not deter Cabot Yerxa, one of the first homesteaders of Desert Hot Springs, to start building his pueblo by hand from scavenged materials in 1941. A true Renaissance man of the desert, Cabot kept adding onto his pueblo until his death in 1965, his patchwork castle having grown as high as four stories with 35 rooms, 150 windows, and 65 doors.

## Moorish Architecture and Arabian Romanticism

Long before Islamic extremism poisoned the perception of the Middle East in the Western world, its image was that of the enchanted world of *Aladdin* and *Arabian Nights*. The fraternal order of the Shriners built grandiose mosque-like edifices in American cities and staged elaborate parades in full Arabian costumes. This fascination was reflected in desert place names. The old stagecoach stop and railroad station of Walters in the Coachella Valley became Mecca. Its hotel was dubbed the Caravansary and the town store became the Bazaar.

Biskra is an ancient city in Algeria known for its date palms. Residential developers chose the name for a palm oasis in the Indio Hills, luring potential land buyers with camel rides to a Bedouin tent camp under the sheltering palms. The enterprise never came to fruition.

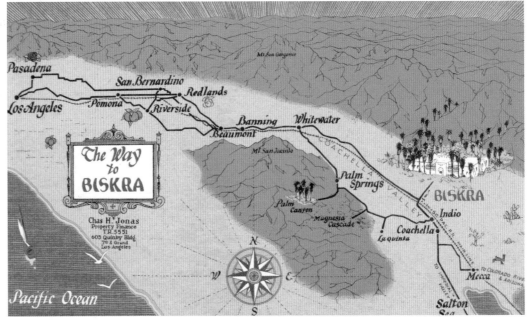

With date farms proliferating in the Coachella Valley, Moorish architecture seemed well suited for the area. The town of Indio hired retired Hollywood art director Harry Oliver to build a skyline of minarets and domes for its annual date festival.

The painter Gordon Coutts came to Palm Springs in 1923 for his health and built Dar Maroc, a home inspired by his trips to Morocco. After his death it became the Gracia Grande apartment hotel and is now the Korakia hotel.

**OPPOSITE:** Mecca and Biskra beckoning big city escapees to the California desert.

**TOP INSET:** A pink Dar Maroc in the 1950s.

**BOTTOM INSET:** The Indio Date Festival pageant.

**RIGHT:** Biskra Palms as it stands today.

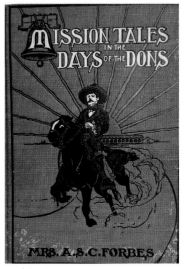

All these escapist visions bore witness to man's search for an alternative to the cramped confines of city life.

What finally succeeded was much closer to the roots and history of the area: A nostalgic look back at the California mission days, purposefully ignoring the padres' role in the suppression of the indigenous population. The names of places and waterways on historical Orange County maps, for example, illustrate the area's ties to Spanish colonial culture. Books and plays like *Ramona* perpetuated this retrospective romance.

**LEFT:** Angelus home brochure for Spanish style homes, 1922.

**RIGHT:** Decorative tiles became a common feature of the Spanish Revival style. The star shape of this fountain points to its origin in the architecture of the 300-year Moorish conquest and reign in Spain.

Los Angeles Sunday Times

Real Estate, Industry and Development

SUNDAY MORNING, AUGUST 14, 1927.

Vol. XLVI.

ARCHITECTURAL PLANS FOR MASTER HOME ACCEPTED

*Spanish Style Designated for "Times" Demonstration Dwelling*

*Typical California Design to Be Followed in Residence on Miramar Estates Site*

The Panama-California Exposition in San Diego introduced Spanish Revival architecture to the public in 1915. In 1927, it was the chosen style for the *Los Angeles Times* model home at the expansive Miramar Estates development and touted as "Typical California design." The building's outline was based on a castle in Sevilla with its painted ceilings being inspired by Moorish motifs in the cathedral of Teruel in Spain.

Tamarisk Road at Palm Canyon Drive, Palm Springs, California

By the 1930s, much of the rapidly expanding Palm Springs was cloaked in the fashionable Spanish Revival style. Hotels like the El Mirador, apartments like the Casa Palmeras, and lavish residences for the wealthy of Las Palmas Estates were built by Los Angeles celebrity architects such as Wallace Neff. Red tile roofs, white stucco walls, and shady verandas dominated the look of "the Village" as it was referred to by locals.

La Plaza shopping center built in 1936 in the heart of the Village is one the best examples of the style in Palm Springs. Despite the center's immense (for the time) size it successfully maintained the feel of a small-town main street plaza.

This block of Tamarisk Road and La Plaza shopping center still retain the Spanish Revival look to this day.

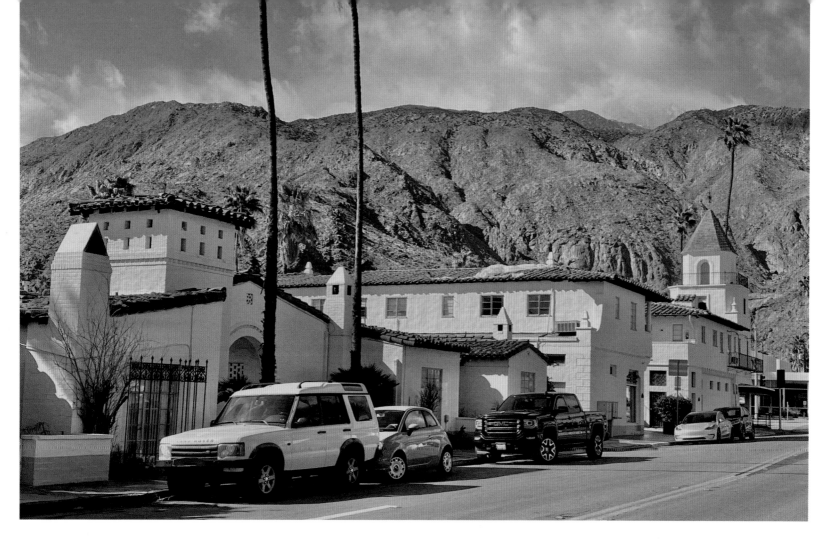

The rustic elegance of Spanish/Mexican haciendas was well suited for the desert environment. Succulents and bougainvillea provided the landscaping, with Mexican fan palms proliferating. Ornamental iron was wrought into gates, railings, and furniture while decorative tiles covered bathrooms, kitchens, and fountains, supporting the mythology of a reimagined past.

Another escapist theme popular in early Palm Springs that continued into the post-World War II era was celebrating the rustic simplicity of the Old West. Horseback riding, cowboy songs around the campfire, and outdoor chuck wagon meals were all accommodated by the warm desert climate. Sweet Singin' Trav Rogers got his Ranch Club going with the enthusiastic support of his friends from the Mink and Manure Club, and the exclusive Smoke Tree Ranch development attracted well-heeled film industry types, like Walt Disney, in search of the simple life.

COWBOY MUSIC AND SONGS
SMOKE TREE RANCH - PALM SPRINGS, CALIF.
FRASHERS FOTO-POMONA

Chuck-Wagon Meal near Palm Springs

Phone 2338
Friendly Horses
ROGERS-RANCH-CLUB
"Where the West Still Lives" PALM SPRINGS, CAL.

COWBOY MUSIC
in the Cantina

BARN DANCES RODEOS

Ranch Club events like the Gold Digger Ball and western wear fashion shows in its knotty pine-lined Wagon Wheel Room became a hub of Palm Springs social life. Weekend rhinestone cowboys amused themselves at festive western barbecue dinners held during the winter season.

**Park your Cadillac and saddle up at the Ranch Club.**

RANCH
CLUB

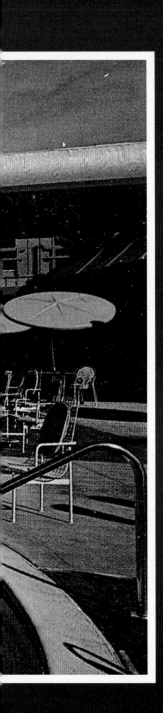

# 2

# OTHER WORLDS TO EXPLORE

## America's Postwar Opening to Foreign Cultures

**B**y the middle of the twentieth century, greater economic freedom and ease fueled a growing curiosity and openness to explore other cultures and travel to exotic ports of call, be they on another continent or in one's hometown.

**OPPOSITE:** The 1962 Asian modern Erawan Garden Hotel in Indian Wells was named after a holy elephant in Hindu Thai mythology.

**ABOVE:** Author Peter Moruzzi and his mother in Japan in 1967.

Theming had been part of American hospitality for some time. To invite the dinner guest to cross the border to another country—where ethnic food and drink were complemented by "authentic" décor—was becoming a favorite activity for a night on the town.

532 GRANT AVE.  SHANGHAI LOW  SAN FRANCISCO, CALIF.
D. W. LOW, Manager

正埠 樓 海 上 金山

FINEST ORIENTAL FOOD
★ The most modern cocktail bar, and lounge. Beautiful scenic murals of China recently completed by Oriental Artists.

COCKTAIL BAR AND LOUNGE

9A-H241

**LEFT**: Proliferating in America's Chinatowns, Chinese restaurants were the first to serve "exotic" food to Americans.

**ABOVE**: Dining rooms not only used furniture and décor, but also murals depicting distant places to enhance their foreign atmosphere.

**OPPOSITE**: Italian, German, Hawaiian, and other themes followed.

The Second World War exposed many Americans to cultures other than their own during their tours of duty. Coming out of the conflict as saviors from global fascism made them feel welcome in previously unfamiliar regions of the planet.

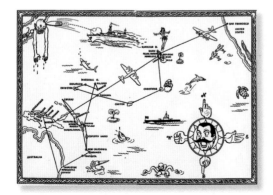

# Have a "Coke" = Kia Ora
### (GOOD LUCK)

## ...or sealing friendships in New Zealand

*Kia ora,* says the New Zealander when he wants to give you his best wishes. It's a down-under way of telling you that you're a pal and that your welfare is a matter of mutual interest. The American soldier says it another way. *Have a "Coke",* says he, and in three words he has made a friend. It's a custom that has followed the flag from the tropics to the polar regions. It's a phrase that says *Welcome, neighbor* from Auckland to Albuquerque, from

New Zealand to New Mexico. 'Round the globe, Coca-Cola stands for *the pause that refreshes,* —has become the high-sign between friendly-minded people.

\* \* \*

*In news stories, books and magazines, you read how much our fighting men cherish Coca-Cola whenever they get it. Yes, more than just a delicious and refreshing drink, "Coke" reminds them of happy times at home. Luckily, they find Coca-Cola —bottled on the spot—in over 35 allied and neutral countries 'round the globe.*

-the global high-sign

"Coke" = Coca-Cola
It's natural for popular names to acquire friendly abbreviations. That's why you hear Coca-Cola called "Coke".

COPYRIGHT 1944, THE COCA-COLA COMPANY

PAPEETE

Nature has been tamed for this tropic hideaway. A waterfall babbles for your pleasure while local wild life stands motionless to keep you at your ease. But spears and pelts remind the diner that the simple life does have its excitements.

SINGAPORE JOE'S
WATERFRONT TAVERN

A gourmet's corner of the Colonies with authenticity as the appetizer. Gas-lit, captain-chaired . . . very British and truly delightful. Your table — once the hatch cover of a ship that proudly carried Her Majesty's flag to far-flung harbors.

MACAO

All the fascinations of foreign sorcery beguile you in this harbor of mystery where the rare sweet-meats of Cathay tempt even the most sophisticated palate. Dine in the gaze of a noble Ming dynasty Kwan-Yin . . . delight in the lavish ebony and mother-of-pearl furnishings. You'll be bewitched!

Saigon

A haven of pleasure . . . dedicated to delights in dining and decor. Rich silks and sacred carvings surround its fortunate inhabitants, heightening their enjoyment in the Oriental offerings. Surrender to the lure of this fascinating city of mystery. It's inevitable!

Stephen Crane expanded his Kon-Tiki restaurant concept into the Ports o' Call, where each of the four dining rooms was inspired by a different Pacific port.

Greater attention was bestowed to the countries of the Pacific Rim. No longer strategic bases, they became exotic vacation destinations—on the map as well as at home. Traveling to faraway places in your own backyard became possible.

THE LIQUID DELIGHTS OF PORTS O'CALL
Both the daring and the demure can sip to their palate's delight! Pictured are three for the intrepid—the South Sea Cooler, the Walking Dead and the Taal. Many unique mixtures of varying potency are offered to those who dare . . .

THE STORY OF THE FOUR PORTS

In another expansion beyond the staid aesthetics of the old world, mid-century homemakers were looking to the Far East to add a note of worldliness to their domiciles. Décor from China and Japan, and rattan furniture imported from the Philippines bestowed an air of international savoir faire on the owners.

This came hand-in-hand with an appreciation of the so-called "primitive" arts of Africa and Oceania. First introduced by avant-garde artists and jazz musicians to America, displaying tribal sculpture added a sparkle of mystery and an aura of adventure to the attractively furnished home.

**TOP:** The Mindoro living room set by Ficks Reed Co.

**RIGHT:** The goddess Kwan Yin joins this atomic family in Lubbock, Texas.

far horizons furniture of romance

Inspired by the Far East, John Wisner designs an exotic group of rattan furniture for modern living. Available at many fine stores. Send 25 cents in coin to Dept. 1. for booklet "Furniture Of Romance".

**Ficks Reed Co.** 424 Findlay Street, Cincinnati 14, Ohio
New York—305 East 63rd St.
Chicago—631 Merchandise Mart  Grand Rapids—Waters Bldg.
Cleveland—1240 Huron Road  San Francisco—431 Jackson Sq.

**TOP RIGHT:** Martin D. May, owner of the May Company Department Store chain, was an avid collector of Oceanic art. In 1963, May advertised a "spectacular exhibition and sale of primitive art from New Guinea of over 1100 pieces from $3 to $3,000."

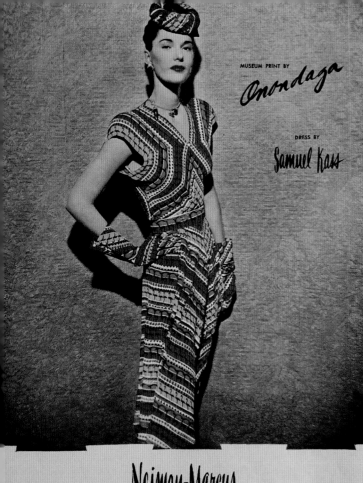

MUSEUM PRINT BY
*Onondaga*

DRESS BY
*Samuel Kass*

*Neiman-Marcus*

TOP LEFT: Neiman-Marcus department store presented this dress by fashion designer Samuel Kass to the public in 1946, incorporating an African "museum print" by Philadelphia's Onondaga silk company.

TOP RIGHT: The cast of the 1962-64 TV show *Hawaiian Eye*—not in Aloha shirts but in Asian silks.

BOTTOM LEFT: Palm Springs' Desert Inn featured Oriental fashions.

BOTTOM RIGHT: Hawaiian-based designer Alfred Shaheen introduced Americans to Mandarin style jackets and Cheongsam dresses.

Satin Brocade
MANDARIN SHEATH
$44.95

DESERT INN
PALM SPRINGS

LAGUNA  BALBOA IS.  WAIKIKI

DIAMOND HEAD SPORTSWEAR

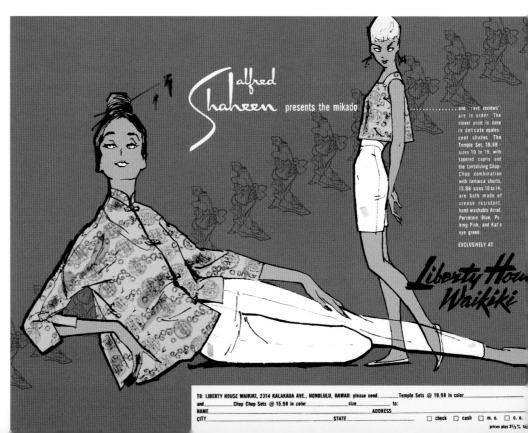

*alfred Shaheen* presents the mikado

and "rave reviews" are in order. The clever print is done in delicate opalescent shades. The Temple Set, 19.98 - sizes 10 to 18, with tapered capris and the tantalizing Chop-Chop combination with Jamaica shorts, 15.98 - sizes 10 to 14, are both made of crease resistant, hand washable Arnel. Porcelain Blue, Peking Pink, and Kat's eye green.

EXCLUSIVELY AT

*Liberty House Waikiki*

TO: LIBERTY HOUSE WAIKIKI, 2314 KALAKAUA AVE., HONOLULU, HAWAII: please send_____ Temple Sets @ 19.98 in color_____
and _____ Chop Chop Sets @ 15.98 in color_____ size_____ to:_____
NAME_____ ADDRESS_____
CITY_____ STATE_____ ☐ check ☐ cash ☐ m. o. ☐ c. o.
prices plus 3½% tax

## Fashion Goes Exotic

Similar to the home décor and hospitality industries, women's fashion also jumped on the non-European bandwagon. Picking up on the trend, various designers introduced whole lines of Asian-style outfits. Hawaii was a classic example of a cultural melting pot made up of the various races of the Pacific Rim and the Western world.

An Invitation to a New Experience

Use Your Head Wear a Krazy Hat.
One of a Kind Originals
- JAMAICA
- AFRICA
- HAITI
- ECUADOR
- SOMOA

Hat Shown $10.00 Incl. Tax & Postage
**KRAZY HATS**
33 THE PLAZA, PALM SPRINGS, CALIF.

**ABOVE:** Part of the spirit of fun in Palm Springs included crazy hat competitions at the annual Easter Hat Parade, which was the inspiration for the store above.

## The Sounds of Faraway Places

Exotic percussion instruments and jazzy vibes provided a soundtrack for the escapist armchair traveler. The advent of hi-fi allowed the creation of an all-enveloping soundscape in one's living room. Hawaii's Martin Denny invented the sound of exotica by adding birdcalls to his multilayered melodies. His eclectic sound became so popular that international flight crews brought him percussion instruments from around the world.

**LEFT:** Martin Denny and his band performing the sound of exotica.

**ABOVE:** Multitalented writer, composer, producer, and bandleader Les Baxter brought the melodies of distant lands into homes.

**OPPOSITE:** East and West met in the music of Japanese composer Tak Shindo.

While international men of mystery traveled to foreign locales on the screen, Americans flocked to Asian restaurants for a taste of exotic adventure. Architecture and décor reflected this desire to experience other cultures. The Ginza Bar at the elaborate Castaway's Resort in South Florida epitomized this trend.

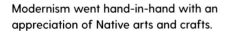

Modernism went hand-in-hand with an appreciation of Native arts and crafts.

From humble mobile homes to sprawling temples of hospitality, Asian Modern abodes invited desert travelers to escape to a different world.

**ABOVE:** The 1962 Erawan Garden Hotel with its swooping A-frame roofs, striking signage, Asian-inspired landscaping, and swimming pool dominated the main highway in Palm Desert.

**FAR RIGHT**: A Chinese-style mobile home at Bing Crosby's Blue Skies Village Mobile Home Park in Rancho Mirage.

ERAWAN GARDEN HOTEL

PALM DESERT • CALIFORNIA

In a setting flanked by exotic plants, in a true Polynesian decor, you may enjoy the absolute ultimate in Cantonese culinary delicacies, accented by authentic tropical drinks. Little wonder that the South Pacific Room is the desert's favorite rendezvous for delightful relaxation.

More than mere atmosphere, the expressive melodies of George Kainapau and his South Sea Island Serenaders will leave you with unforgettable memories. For here is Island music played and sung by native experts, with its full complement of colorful nuances, its true Hawaiian flavor.

*"Beneath the Tower of the Stars"*

**ABOVE:** An advertisement for the South Pacific Room in *Palm Springs Villager* magazine.

**RIGHT:** The menu for the El Mirador Hotel's South Pacific Room that opened following the hotel's remodel in 1952.

# 3

# POLYNESIA IN THE DESERT

By the 1950s, with the various influences and inspirations from foreign lands, one recreational lifestyle began to stand out. Hawaii and Polynesia had long exerted a fascination as a dream destination for Americans. Polynesian culture seemed to offer more possibilities for fun and games in fashion, festivities, and dining out (with copious amounts of tropical cocktails). Of all the other themes that had preceded it, the idea of escaping to the South Pacific appeared as the most liberating. In Palm Springs, nothing signified the changing of the public's taste more than the Spanish-style El Mirador Hotel opening its South Pacific Room in 1952.

IN THE GARDEN, EL MIRADOR HOTEL, PALM SPRINGS, CALIFORNIA          3A-H539

The El Mirador—jewel of the Spanish Revival in the desert.

Ever since their discovery, the Polynesian islands conveyed the image of an earthly paradise. This was perpetuated in novels, movies, and music. The island way of life—happy natives frolicking on tropical beaches, minimally clad due to the balmy climate and free of the stresses of civilization—appeared as a desirable alternative to the 9-to-5 drudgery of the average American. Indulging in this dream became a favorite form of leisure.

**LEFT:** The romantic vision of a South Sea island garden of Eden.

**OPPOSITE LEFT:** A rare color photo of Pago Pago in Palm Springs, circa 1943.

**OPPOSITE TOP RIGHT:** Hollywood's depiction of a sumptuous island feast with westerners as honored guests.

Hawaii, practically in America's backyard, was the most familiar part of Polynesia, and thus a symbol of that dream. People wanted to be where fun and whimsy could be had. While initially visiting these islands was out of reach for the average citizen, an easy alternative was found in the local Polynesian watering hole. The Waikiki nightclub of Palm Springs, which soon became the Pago Pago, was one of the first tropical hideaways in the village. It not only attracted the average tourist but celebrities like industrialist Howard Hughes, movie stars Dorothy Lamour, Douglas Fairbanks Jr., producer Daryl Zanuck, and director Howard Hawks.

The Hotel Lexington in New York City started a trend that would affect the spread of Polynesian lounges across America. In 1937, the Lexington opened the Hawaiian Room as the first major show-room for live Hawaiian entertainment in the U.S. It featured the lilting melodies of Lani McIntire and his Aloha Islanders supported by a dance troupe of beautiful Hawaiian hula dancers.

The nightclub soon became known as the eastern outpost of Hawaii, and its success prompted other hotels to open Polynesian rooms. Within a few years any hotel worth its salt had to have its own tropical hideaway. On the opposite coast, the historic Mission Inn in Riverside, California, converted its Chinese dining room into the Lea Lea Supper Club.

A Scene from RODGERS and HAMMERSTEIN'S "SOUTH PACIFIC"
A MAGNA Production
Produced by BUDDY ADLER    Color by DELUXE    Released by 20th CENTURY-FOX
Printed in the U.S.A.

In Palm Springs, the Spanish Colonial Revival-style hotel El Mirador followed the trend with its South Pacific Room. The name was inspired by the triumphant musical *South Pacific* that had a major influence on increasing public awareness of Polynesian style in America. Several songs from the musical's songbook became hit records such as "Bali Hai," "Some Enchanted Evening," and "Happy Talk," performed by the top performers of the time. A major Hollywood motion picture followed, perpetuating the spell of the South Pacific on America.

The South Pacific Room became one of the most popular nightclubs in Palm Springs where tourists and celebrities such as Bing Crosby and Jerry Lewis went native by coming attired in South Sea island fashions or in beachcomber style. Entertainment was provided by George Kainapau, the "songbird of Hawaii," and his island serenaders. Performing with them was "Tahitian Goddess of the Dance, lovely Tani Marsh." The South Pacific Room's luau feasts and Hawaiian fashion shows always attracted a sizable crowd.

A major draw at all Polynesian-style establishments was the tropical cocktails, and the El Mirador was no exception. It invited guests to "sip those soothing delectable South Sea Island concoctions" such as the Head Hunter, Witches Brew, Typhoon, and Desert Cooler. In fact, the Bogert's Downfall cocktail was named for the club's manager, all around bon vivant, and future Palm Springs mayor Frank Bogert.

**ABOVE TOP:** Interior of the South Pacific Room.

**ABOVE:** Lovely Tani Marsh beckons.

**OPPOSITE:** Delectable concoctions awaited the parched desert dweller.

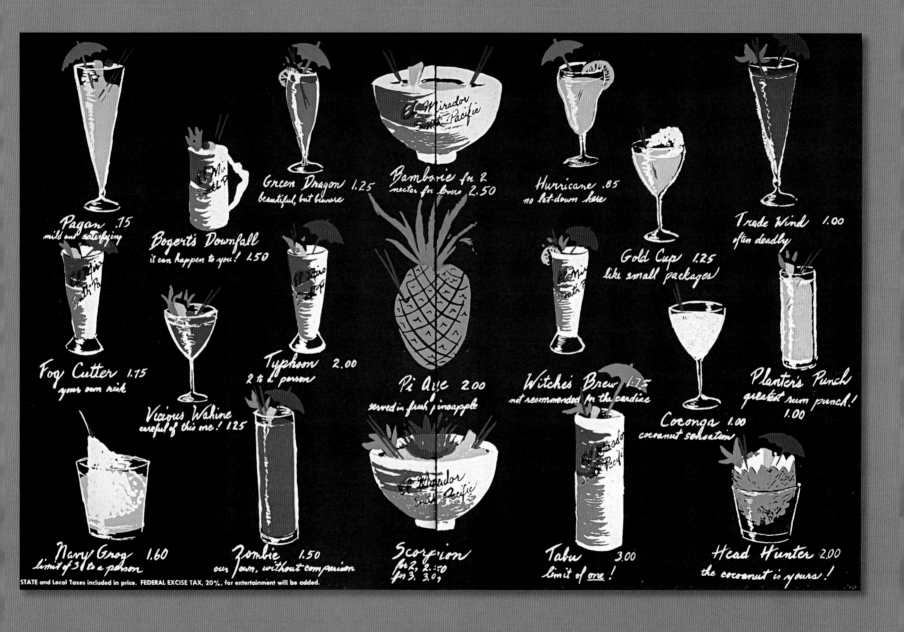

Pagan .15
mild and satisfying

Bogert's Downfall
it can happen to you! 1.50

Green Dragon 1.25
beautiful, but beware

Bamboie for 2
nectar for lovers 2.50

Hurricane .85
no let-down here

Trade Wind 1.00
often deadly

Fog Cutter 1.75
your own risk

Vicious Wahine
careful of this one! 1.25

Typhoon 2.00
2 to a person

Pi Aie 2.00
served in fresh pineapple

Gold Cup 1.25
like small packages

Witches Brew 1.75
not recommended for the cardiac

Coconga 1.00
coconut sensation

Planter's Punch
greatest rum punch!
1.00

Navy Grog 1.60
limit of 3 to a person

Zombie 1.50
our own, without companion

Scorpion
for 2, 2.50
for 3, 3.00

Tabu 3.00
limit of one !

Head Hunter 2.00
the coconut is yours !

STATE and Local Taxes included in price. FEDERAL EXCISE TAX, 20%, for entertainment will be added.

Architect and proprietor Hank Gogerty's Desert Air Hotel combined modernism and an innovative fly-in concept with the exotic appeal of the hotel's Luau Hut cocktail lounge.

For Luncheon, Dinner, Cocktails...

## COMPASS ROOM & LUAU HUT

*Nightly Entertainment*

### 200 ACRES OF SUN AND FUN!

| | | |
|---|---|---|
| Swimming | Riding | Chuckwagon Breakfasts |
| Sunbathing | Sightseeing | Moonlight Rides |
| Dancing | Airplane Rides | Bar and Cocktail Lounge |

### FOR RESERVATIONS—
TELEPHONE PALM DESERT 76-2581

*Desert Air* HOTEL AND COTTAGES

PALM DESERT AIRPARK, 10 MILES SOUTH OF PALM SPRINGS, CALIFORNIA

**OPPOSITE:** The bamboo-clad Luau Hut offered "pleasant potions."

**TOP LEFT:** The hotel's Lanai Suites featured rattan furniture and tropical prints galore.

**LEFT:** View onto the plane parking lot from the Compass Room.

Hank Gogerty utilized the vast expanse of the property's airfield to organize annual luau events. According to a 1954 article in the *Desert Sun*, it was "A luau of such heroic proportions that it will go down in history as the greatest ever staged in the desert." The article continued, "a vast expanse of the adjacent airfield [was used] to organize the largest luau events of the season. A pit will be lined with lava rock and a pig and yams will be roasted island fashion." Wonderful Tahitian rum punch put guests in the mood for the evening's festivities.

Make Reservations Now for
HANK GOGERTY'S 6th ANNUAL DESERT AIR

# Hawaiian Luau

SATURDAY EVENING MAY 24, 1958

Exotic tropical food cooked in the underground imu.
Fresh flower leis from Hawaii for the ladies.
Dress: Hawaiian or informal.

## NATIVE HAWAIIAN ENTERTAINMENT

*featuring the beloved*

**HILO HATTIE**
**GEORGE KAINAPAU**
"The Golden Voice of Hawaii"

Kahulu Lucy     Toot Marsh
Hawaiian        Tahitian

*Interpretations*

**FRED LETULI and LANI**
*in the spectacular*
**Samoan Knife and Fire Dance**
**BILL WHISLING**
*Famous Hawaiian Comedian*
**CARLYLE & HIS ORCHESTRA**

Danny Santos          Pineapple Pete
Lovely Hawaiian and Tahitian Dancers and Entertainers
**JUNGLE DRUMS CEREMONY**
*featuring the great*
**THURSTON KNUDSON**

TICKETS
$12.50
EACH

*including* TAHITIAN
RUM PUNCH 7 to 8 p.m.
THE LUAU FEAST
ENTERTAINMENT
DANCING  *Tax and Tips*
Sponsorship: Desert Air Club

*Fly to*

**Desert Air**
HOTEL

PALM DESERT AIRPARK
PALM SPRINGS, CALIF.

Phone—FAirview 2-3131 in Palm Springs,
Fireside 6-4127 in Palm Desert
Los Angeles office, DUnkirk 5-6756

DESERT AIR LUAU HOST HANK
GOGERTY twirls Ruby Meyers in his
own interpretation of a Hawaiian ceremonial dance. Hank was his usual
inimitable self as he went through his
now-traditional 'Keep Your Hands on
the Eyes' routine to the accompaniment
of Hilo Hattie.

**TOP LEFT:** Blessing over the imu (a traditional earth oven) performed by a Hawaiian kahuna. Gogerty, with arms folded, stands next to Hilo Hattie who's wearing one of her famous muumuus.

**ABOVE:** Tantalizing 1958 advertisement for the Desert Air luau.

**FAR LEFT:** Luau guests getting in the swing of the Hawaiian hula.

PALM SPRINGS, CALIFORNIA

PALM SPRINGS HOTEL

CLOSE COVER BEFORE STRIKING

The Luau

TROPICAL DRINKS
CANTONESE FOOD

The Luau restaurant in the Palm Springs Hotel preceded the popularity of the luau festivity as the favorite event theme in the desert. Originating in Hawaii, the luau was the highlight of the tourist experience in the islands and spread to the mainland after World War II. During the four months of "season" in Palm Springs, the reigning social set as well as the local villagers had ample time on their hands to plan and decorate events, and the luau became the party format of choice.

**ABOVE:** The Palm Springs Luau was a favorite of Hollywood personalities such as Rudy Vallee, Harold Lloyd, and Peter Lorre.

**RIGHT:** A classic tourist luau at the beach in Waikiki.

Luau fun (and profit) proved to be infectious to the Palm Springs hospitality industry. It got to the point where every hotel, country club, social organization, and even local high schools featured a festive luau as entertainment. *Palm Springs Life* magazine celebrated the advent of The Luau Season on its cover.

LET'S HAVE A LUAU

Social club events and private parties gave women the opportunity to wear the latest and brightest in Hawaiian fashion. Gentlemen got in on the act by sporting an infinite variety of aloha shirt patterns at Polynesian soirées, with both sexes adorned with the customary flower leis.

## Hundreds Attend Pied Pipers Luau

### DHS Fete At Mobile Home Park

By ELLEN SAUNDERS

The 350 people fortunate enough to have purchased tickets for the 1966 luau held by the Pied Pipers of Desert Hot Springs were practically unanimous in their opinion that this was "the best one ever."

Certainly it was the largest. Although all the tickets were sold, a long line of people came out to Desert Crest Mobilhomes hoping that they could be admitted. Mrs. Dennis Thorson, club president, obliged, hoping that the food would hold out and it did.

The setting at the Desert Crest Clubhouse was perfect. Tables on the sheltered patio and in the recreation hall proved ample for the guests. There was no crowding thanks to the spacious surroundings, and Hoot Gibson and his "Hawaiian people. Hampered by a crowd

LUAU GUESTS — Mrs. Jack Morey, left, stops to talk with Mr. and Mrs. Willard McKinney, among the many men and women who enjoyed the Polynesian food and entertainment throughout the evening at the luau.

GIFT — Mrs. Dennis Thorson presents Clifford Bloch with a Hawaiian lei at the Pied Piper as Mrs. Russel Driggers, left, talks with Mrs. Bloch. The Polynesian party was held at Desert Crest Mobilhomes. Halberts, Mrs. Robert Pritchard, wild, chatted awhile with friends

**OPPOSITE:** Ladies of the luau at the El Mirador hotel pool.

**BELOW:** The luau exemplified the consumer abundance of the 1950s.

**RIGHT:** A luau party for the guests of the General Realty Company at the Halekulani Apartments in Palm Desert.

*A TYPICAL HAWAIIAN LUAU was the scene of the announcement of the appointment of Holiday Realty Corporation as the exclusive agents for General Realty Company for the sale of one acre homesites in Hawaiian Paradise Park on the Island of Hawaii. Mr. Herb Hall, President of General Realty explained the various facets of the newest Hawaiian subdivision during the festivities and Dick Coffin, General Manager of Holiday Realty gathered his sales staff for the occasion at the newly opened Halekulani Apartments in Palm Desert.*

GEORGE
**ALLARDICE**
entertains nightly in the
intimate setting of the
Lahaina Room. Great tropical
drinks, lush tropical décor.

THE
**GUADALAJARA** BOYS
entertain in the
Vista Lounge, playing music of
yesterday and today, for your
listening and dancing pleasure.

The Terrace Room-Excellent cuisine with view.

*Jerry Buss'* **OCOTILLO LODGE**
1111 East Palm Canyon Drive Palm Springs, Calif 92262 (714) 327-1141

With their tropical environs, South Seas cocktail bars were a good fit for the recreation destination of Palm Springs because such establishments were an extension of the town's spirit of escapism. By embodying the idea of "getting away from it all," the Lahaina Room, Luau, Bali Bali, Kon Tiki, Waikiki, Chi Chi, Pago Pago, and Zanzibar offered a vacation within a vacation.

**ABOVE:** The ultramodern Ocotillo Lodge was home to the Lahaina Room decorated in primitive décor by Oceanic Arts of Whittier, California.

**RIGHT:** The Bali Bali at the Royal Palms Hotel was an early South Seas bar/restaurant favored by winter colonists and villagers.

**OPPOSITE:** The journey of the raft Kon-Tiki from Peru to Polynesia inspired Tiki lounges across America including Palm Springs.

# + 4 +
# THE CHI CHI
# NIGHTCLUBS

**M**erry-making in colorful garb in the temperate desert climate was one thing, but Palm Springs villagers still wanted to go out on the town in style. The Chi Chi fulfilled that need as the most elegant and sophisticated nightclub in the desert.

---

**OPPOSITE:** The Chi Chi's famous Starlite Room.

**RIGHT:** Dapper Chi Chi owner Irwin Schuman switches roles with comedian Jerry Lewis playing the host, holding the club's iconic menu.

By the late 1950s, the Chi Chi was architecturally the chicest, most modern night spot in Palm Springs, attracting the same stable of stars as glamorous Las Vegas. The roster of famous performers added to the reputation of Palm Springs as a magnet for celebrities, complementing its status as a recreational destination for the Hollywood elite.

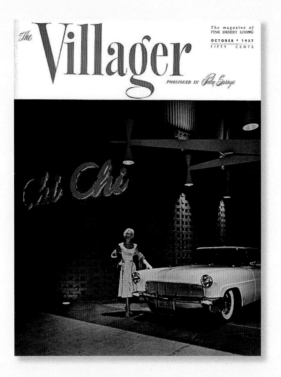

The Villager
*The magazine of* FINE DESERT LIVING
OCTOBER • 1957
FIFTY CENTS
PUBLISHED IN *Palm Springs*

Chi Chi

Chi Chi

♦ Chi Chi Lounge

Grill Room ♦

Patio

Surroundings of luxurious elegance for Luncheon, Dinner and Supper

Choicest Foods expertly prepared
•
Open daily
11 a.m. to 2 a.m.

**OPPOSITE AND ABOVE:** The lineup of top stars of stage and screen at the Chi Chi successfully matched the biggest showrooms of Las Vegas.

**LEFT:** The Chi Chi provided multiple drinking and dining experiences in distinctive rooms throughout the enormous establishment.

# Chi-Chi

## Starlite Room

The origin of the Chi Chi name was inspired by a black velvet portrait of a topless Tahitian woman, known as Hina Rapa. Her cheerful expression exuded such a captivating joie de vivre that proprietor Irwin Schuman chose her image as the logo icon for the nightclub. Hina Rapa's exceptional beauty had been captured by artist Edgar Leeteg in black velvet. Schuman reproduced her image on everything: dishware, ashtrays, matchbooks, swizzle sticks, playing cards, photo folders, and, of course, on its menu. Leeteg famously stated that the nightclub used his painting without permission, disparaging the Chi Chi as "a Hollywood gin mill."

German émigré Edgar Leeteg arrived in Tahiti in 1933. First working as a sign painter, he began to create sensuous portraits of local women on black velvet, selling them to enthusiastic tourists who brought them back to mainland America. Leeteg was the pioneer of black velvet nudes as a staple of Tiki bar décor. His portrait of Hina Rapa was easily his most successful work and he did not hesitate to create multiple versions of it during his illustrious career.

**OPPOSITE:** Seven Seas proprietor Bob Brooks was one of the earliest patrons of Leeteg. Others like Don the Beachcomber followed suit.

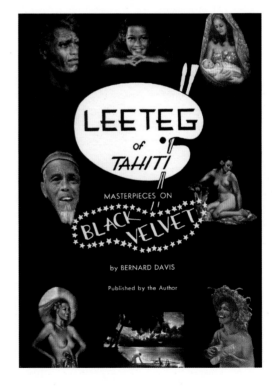

Bob Brooks'

7 SEAS

6904 Hollywood Boulevard
Hollywood 28, California, U. S. A.
Opposite Grauman's Chinese Theatre

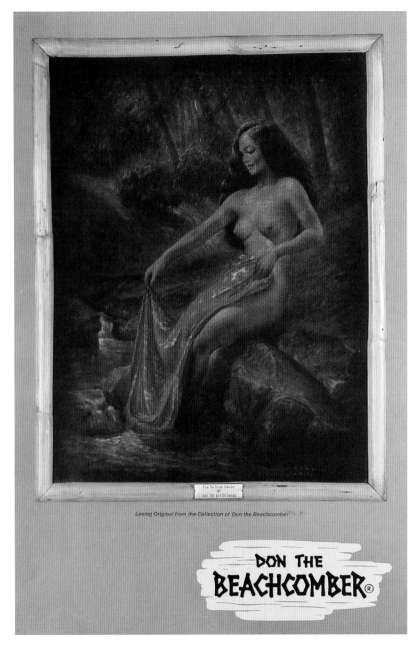

Leeteg Original from the Collection of Don the Beachcomber

DON THE
BEACHCOMBER®

## Dining with Nudes— an American Tradition

Decorating the walls of dining rooms with portraits of female nudes was not as unusual as one might think nowadays. The custom originated with Howard Chandler Christy's murals of nude nymphs at the Café Des Artistes in New York in 1934 and continued with Charlie Anderson's Domino Club in San Francisco. This broadminded use of artistic nudity projected a bohemian atmosphere for the adult clientele, male and female alike. The décor concept spread to the walls of cocktail lounges and upscale dining rooms throughout the country.

As part of the fantasy of the Polynesian paradise, the entrancing hula girl had always been one of the symbols of the escapist qualities of island culture. Her nudity was evocative of the carefree South Seas life and she was portrayed on menus, murals, and mugs.

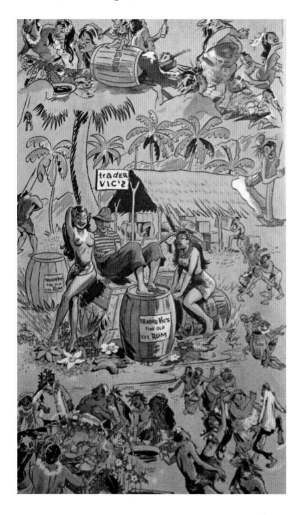

**ABOVE:** The bandstand back mural painted by Frank Bowers at Zamboanga Club, Los Angeles.

**FAR LEFT:** The classic Trader Vic's menu portraying the uninhibited reverie of native celebrations.

**LEFT:** A ceramic mug/ashtray for "The Body" cocktail served at Sugie's Tropics, Beverly Hills.

## From Desert to Island— Chi Chi Expansion

Like many successful restaurateurs before him, Irwin Schuman had big plans for expanding the Chi Chi brand. At one point his efforts reached as far as Catalina Island off the Southern California coast. The island's isthmus had been famous for its Christian's Hut bar since the on-location filming of *Mutiny on the Bounty* in 1935. Schuman widened the sand beaches, planted new palm trees, and converted the old dance pavilion into the local Chi Chi. Unfortunately, the advent of World War II resulted in all tourism to Catalina being halted and the isthmus commandeered as a training ground for the U.S. Coast Guard.

The many other Chi Chi outposts managed by Schuman such as Belmont Shore and Riverside had equally short lives. Chi Chi Palm Springs endured as a favorite Village gathering place for decades.

# ✦ 5 ✦
# THE LOOK OF TIKI:
## Waltah Clarke

**W**altah Clarke was the enthusiastic ambassador of Polynesian style in California and Hawaii. With Palm Springs as his base, his Hawaiian-wear shops proliferated in resort towns and vacation destinations in the Southwest. Waltah's sense of humor and colorful use of the Hawaiian language personified the spirit of aloha.

**OPPOSITE:** Waltah Clarke opened his first shop in Palm Springs in 1952.

A young Walter Clarke arrived in Hawaii in the late 1930s. By eventually working as a manager for Trader Vic's and then as publicity manager for Don the Beachcomber he got his education in the art of popularizing Hawaiian culture for the burgeoning tourist trade. In 1951, Clarke got the job to write a humorous column for the *Honolulu Advertiser* newspaper as its beach correspondent. Clarke wrote from "the third umbrella on the left" on the beach at Waikiki, befriending the local beachboys who worked for the big Hawaiian hotels giving surfing lessons and outrigger rides to visitors. The popular column was soon syndicated by newspapers across the United States.

# On the Beach at Waikiki

★ ★ ★ ★ ★ ★ ★

## *Who's Who Gossip in Sand and Surf*

### By WALTER CLARKE

(Mr. Clarke is Waikiki columnist for the Los Angeles Times, The San Francisco Chronicle, the Seattle Post-Intelligencer and the Sydney, Australia, Daily Telegraph.)

Great thing about Hawaii is—even when the weather's bad, it's good compared with some spots we can think of. But Bruddah! did Waikiki ever look like a throwback to "Rain" a while there! Even Panama's outrigger canoe was flying the distress signal. But that didn't bother the coast folk and here's a few we bumped into while bumming around the beach:

Those Washingtonians Mr. and Mrs. Joseph Gardner, the Charles S. Wills, the R. A. Willetts and the W. L. Wordons, Mr. and Mrs. George Gunn Jr., Max and Mrs. Silver and Mr. and Mrs. W. E. McElfatrick. Some fun, huh, Brother Elfatrick? But really! It's kinda funny in Waikiki when it rains. Everybody wants their money back (so we pay 'em in

**Mr. Clarke**

ers (Riverside), John Foster, Harriet Lewis. And the good Doctor and Mrs. John Boyd of Stagecoach Gulch—Tucson, Arizona. And another cute group: Martha and Omar Fareed (who knows a lot of our pals like Elaine and Bill Hollingsworth and Doug and Dorothy Belle Kennaston— and they OUGHTA know Juanita and Jack Giba!).

★ ★ ★

Over there's Deirdre and Don Budge (good name—can't budge him from the beach) and Margaret and Cliff Capps. Sounds just like Santa Monica Beach, doesn't it? And another: Lou Miller, the Bankamerica Vip. Gotta cute wife,

**FAR LEFT:** Walter showing a visitor how to have fun.

**LEFT:** Walter Clarke, Waikiki Beach correspondent.

**ABOVE:** Walter learning from Don the Beachcomber.

**OPPOSITE:** Waltah Clarke with surfing legend Duke Kahanamoku (top row, second from right) and beachboy buddies.

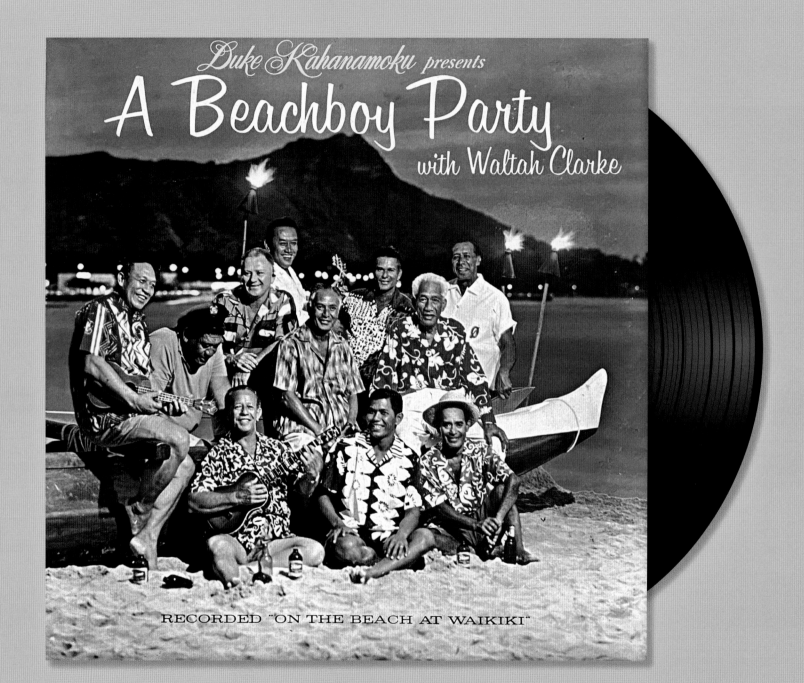

Clarke's friendship with the beachboys taught him to how to speak Hawaiian Pidgeon English, which he would use in humorous ways to promote his galaxy of clothing shops, referring to himself henceforth as Waltah Clarke.

**ABOVE:** Waltah (top left), wife Gretchen, and friends sporting colorful aloha wear at a Palm Springs luau.

**RIGHT AND OPPOSITE:** Waltah employed his Waikiki beachboy cred by featuring the pop poetry of Hawaiian Pigeon English in his advertisements.

# on the Beach at Waikiki
## By WALTER CLARKE

Waltah tapped into America's love for Hawaii and the South Pacific by importing aloha wear as the costume for escaping the conservative patterns of American daily life.

By managing the business aspects of the company, Waltah Clarke's wife, Gretchen, was an important part of the growth of the brand. Focusing on vacation and holiday destinations, their chain of shops expanded to dozens of locations, including Disneyland. Having started out with a small shop in El Mirador Hotel in Palm Springs, the Waltah Clarke name eventually returned to the islands by opening shops in numerous Hawaiian hotels.

**Waltah Clarke's**
**HAWAIIAN SHOPS**

| | |
|---|---|
| ANAHEIM — | Disneyland Hotel Plaza |
| BALBOA ISLAND — | 209 Marine Ave. |
| BEVERLY HILLS — | 367 N. Beverly Dr. |
| CATALINA — | 423 Crescent St. |
| CORAL GABLES — | 345 Miracle Mile |
| FT. LAUDERDALE — | 812 E. Las Olas Blvd. |
| GLENDALE — | 239 N. Glendale Ave. |
| HONOLULU — | 2217 Ala Moana Center |
| HONOLULU — | Outrigger Hotel |
| LAGUNA BEACH — | 265 Forest Ave. |
| LA JOLLA — | 7933 Girard Ave. |
| LAS VEGAS — | 3041 Las Vegas Blvd., S. |
| LOS ANGELES — | Airport Marina Hotel |
| MONTEREY — | Del Monte Center |
| NEWPORT BEACH — | 26 Fashion Island |
| PALM BEACH — | 225 Worth Ave. |
| PALM SPRINGS — | 136 S. Palm Canyon Dr. |
| PALM SPRINGS — | 466 S. Palm Canyon Dr. |
| PALM SPRINGS — | Tropics Hotel |
| PASADENA — | 268 S. Lake Ave. |
| PHOENIX — | 4431 E. Thomas Rd. |
| SANTA ANA — | Bullock's Fashion Sq. |
| SANTA BARBARA — | 3825 State St. |
| SCOTTSDALE — | 4500 N. Scottsdale Rd. |

**WALTAH AND GRETCHEN** Clarke today are greeting Villagers and friends in their new Hawaiian shop at 136 South Palm Canyon Drive. The formal opening is today and everyone is invited. The new shop, fourth location of the Clarkes' in Southern California, features $50,000 in South Sea Island wear of all makes and descriptions.

**OPPOSITE:** Waltah Clarke's flagship store on Palm Canyon Drive. Eventually Waltah operated three stores in Palm Springs.

Waltah Clarke was actively involved in Palm Springs civic, social, and commercial life. Advertised as the "white boy gone native," he hosted luaus and numerous fashion shows at local hotels. Organizing Hawaiian-themed charity benefits, he also took on the role of presiding over the town's renowned Desert Circus parade. A long-standing parade tradition was female sheriffs issuing citations to anyone not wearing Western or Hawaiian wear.

2nd annual
Hawaiian Festival Week
1966 PROGRAM

**LEFT:** A poolside fashion show featuring Waltah Clarke's latest designs.

**ABOVE:** One of Waltah's projects was Hawaiian Festival Week also known as Aloha Week.

**OPPOSITE:** Waltah Clarke's joyful Desert Circus float cruises down Palm Canyon Drive.

Waltah Clarke's introduction of aloha fashion from the islands contributed to Hawaiian wear becoming the dominant look of leisure for generations of Americans. People were able to express their individuality by choosing among an endless variety of bright colors and abstract patterns.

### Indubitably the Palm Springs look

Cool, casually super. Intrepid short sleeve bush jacket of a comfortable summer cotton batik print, in a choice of blue, green or gold. **15.00.** The pants, by Lancer, in Dacron® polyester knit, are styled in a slim beltless model with top pockets…a star performer in faultless fit and comfort. They're machine washable, never need ironing; no bagging ever for their shape retention is tops. White, blue, gold, green **22.50**

## SILVERWOODS
DESERT INN FASHION PLAZA 155 No. Palm Canyon Drive

**OPPOSITE:** A strikingly modern petroglyph design in bold colors by Waltah Clarke.

**ABOVE:** Interior designer and fashion plate Carlos Kiko Cardoza modeling several examples of "The Palm Springs Look" from his vintage aloha shirt collection.

# 6

# CLIF AND LOU SAWYER—
## Premiere Purveyors of Polynesian Pop

**B**eginning with the Bali Bali restaurant in 1949 in Palm Springs, and continuing with the Chi Chi, South Pacific Room, and Don The Beachcomber, the architecture and design couple of Clif and Lou Sawyer had a hand in many of the bamboo temples mentioned in the previous chapters. Although they made their home in Palm Springs in 1951 while maintaining an office in Los Angeles, their influence on Tiki style in America went far beyond the desert.

---

**OPPOSITE:** Clif and Lou Sawyer at The Lanai, San Mateo.

**RIGHT:** Rendering for the proposed Ports O' Seven Seas in Palm Springs.

The Sawyers advanced the molding and shaping of bamboo and rattan into an art form. The tropical watering holes of entrepreneur Joe Chastek were a perfect example of exotic jungle huts transferred into the big city. The Zamboanga was named after a city in the Philippines. Vagabond's House was taken from a poem and bestselling book by Hawaii's poet laureate Don Blanding.

Joe Chastek's Zamboanga was a classic South Seas nightclub in Los Angeles.

Before the Tiki figure became the symbol of Polynesian Pop in America, the American South Seas fantasy was inhabited by hula girls, palm trees, and bamboo. Clif and Lou Sawyer were masters at creating a floor-to-ceiling environment of tropical textures.

Inspired by a Don Blanding poem, the Vagabond's House featured images of native nudes and the Sawyers' trademark angled bamboo posts held together by rope lashing.

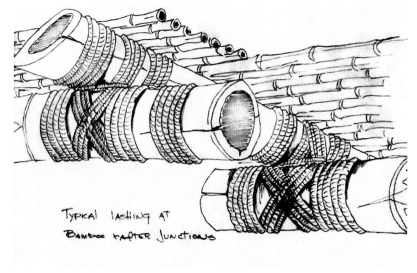

The Sawyers' body of work spread far beyond Southern California to tropical-themed establishments in places such as Oregon, Arizona, Wyoming, and Alaska. Another design feature employed by the couple was the Chinese lotus tile introduced by Don the Beachcomber.

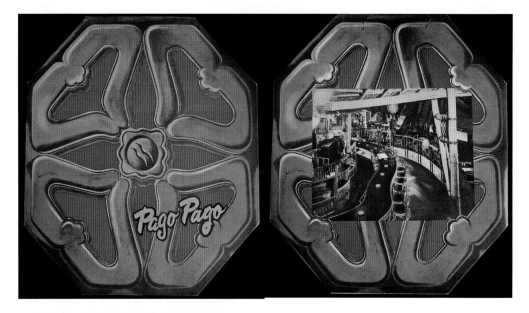

**TOP:** Menu from the Pago Pago in Portland.

**LEFT:** Pago Pago Portland interior.

**ABOVE:** Matchbook cover from the Tucson Pago Pago.

Tropical escapes were welcome in snowy climes like Alaska and Wyoming.

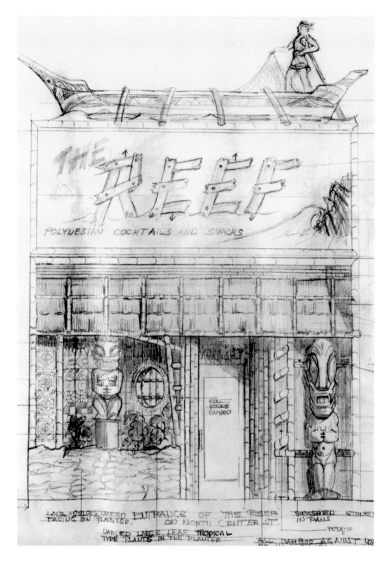

**TOP LEFT**: Bears and prospectors mingling with hula dancers in Anchorage, Alaska.

**ABOVE:** The blueprint for The Reef in Casper, Wyoming, by Clif Sawyer.

Among the Sawyers' many creations were important Tiki temples such as The Lanai in San Mateo, California, and The Luau in Beverly Hills.

---

**RIGHT:** The blueprint for beachcomber-style light fixtures for The Lanai.

**BOTTOM:** A sprawling native village emerges in San Mateo.

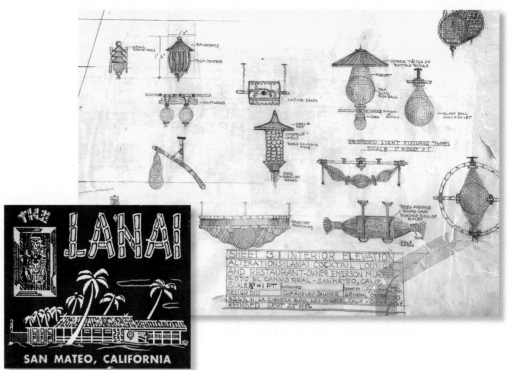

A magnificent layered glass diorama set in the back bar of The Lanai featured remarkable day-to-night lighting effects.

A significant power place in the evolution of Tiki style, The Luau in Beverly Hills displayed another feature of the Sawyer style in its conical entrance hut topped by a Tiki totem. The Luau's logo Tiki was designed by Clif Sawyer, appearing in many of his renderings.

Proposed "LUAU" AT LAS VEGAS, NEV. by Clif Sawyer

**OPPOSITE:** The entrance to The Luau in Beverly Hills.

**ABOVE:** A detailed blueprint for a proposed Luau in Las Vegas.

**RIGHT:** The Luau logo Tiki on the matchbook and salt and pepper shakers.

THE LUAU

421 N. RODEO BEVERLY HILLS

CLOSE COVER BEFORE STRIKING MATCH

Besides restaurants, the Sawyers also designed the Beachcomber Shops in Palm Springs. They coexisted with Waltah Clarke's Hawaiian Shops, signifying that South Seas fashions remained the dominant style of resort wear in the desert.

Men's
Women's
Children's

Shirts
Shorts
Swim Wear

Blouses
Skirts
Play Wear
Dresses

Authentic
Hawaiian
Jewelry

Exotic
Island
Scents

*It's Our Way of Saying*

*Thank You*

To Celebrate the Opening of our Second

*Beachcomber Shop*

which you, our many friends, made possible . . . all our exquisite new stock is being sold at 25% discount until Monday, October 26th.

Of course, after Monday everything will be sold at regular prices.

*Beachcomber Shops*

276 N. Palm Canyon Drive
Phone 4012

187 S. Palm Canyon Drive
Phone 5506

Several celebrity desert residents were quite invested in the growth of the Palm Springs area. Crooner Bing Crosby organized friends into financing a new development to be built on the outskirts of Palm Springs, in what would eventually become Rancho Mirage, called Blue Skies Trailer Village. Christened "America's Most Luxurious Trailer Park," many of the trailers were whimsically customized in various themes including Egyptian, American Colonial, and Chinese. The Sawyers brought their South Seas style to the mundane mobile home genre by dressing their friend Elona Seagrave's trailer in Tiki style. Lou Sawyer proudly asserted, "I have just created the first tropical décor in trailers in the country."

For a while, Clif and Lou Sawyer operated a tropical décor shop in Cathedral City. Their most important work in Palm Springs was the renovation and expansion of the beloved Don the Beachcomber on Palm Canyon Drive in 1962. Their artistry was praised in local articles that dubbed the pair "the scintillating Sawyers." After Clif passed away in 1966, Lou continued to design themed spaces in restaurants, shops, and homes.

**LEFT:** Lou places a lei around one of their custom-designed Tikis.

**OPPOSITE:** The blueprint for the expanded Don the Beachcomber.

**OPPOSITE INSET:** The gas Tiki torches remain atop the long departed Don the Beachcomber on Palm Canyon Drive.

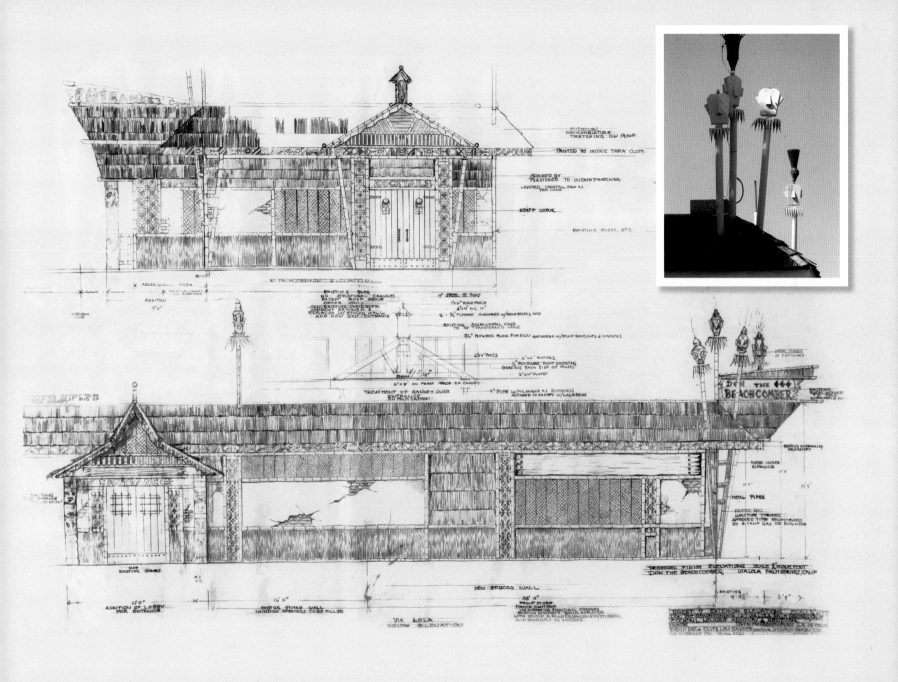

# 7

# DON THE BEACHCOMBER—
## A Palm Springs Institution

**D**on the Beachcomber can be considered the founding father of Polynesian Pop. The canon of tropical cocktails that he invented in the 1930s formed the foundation of the Tiki mixology that spread throughout the Polynesian restaurant and bar industry. From his home base in Hollywood, his hospitality concept grew to various locations including Palm Springs.

**OPPOSITE:** The Palm Springs Don the Beachcomber opened in 1953 and was expanded in 1962.

**PI YI**

Crushed fresh Hawaiian fruits and light Cuban Rums served in a hollowed-out baby pineapple.

**TAHITIAN RUM PUNCH**

Exotic tropical fruits admirably blended with Mexican limes and old Cuban Rums

From his travels in the South Pacific and Jamaica, Don had developed a penchant for rum and a knack for mixing tropical flavors into new delectable concoctions that quickly proved to be popular with the Hollywood set. Don was familiar with the film community from working as an advisor on South Seas movies. After renting the souvenirs and mementos he had collected on his voyages to the studios, he proceeded to decorate his beachcomber cafe with these exotic objects, creating the bohemian atmosphere of a Pacific port watering hole.

THE BEACHCOMBER CAFE    FAMOUS NIGHT SPOT    HOLLYWOOD, CAL. 49

**TOP:** Don with some of his creations.

**ABOVE:** The original 1934 Don the Beachcomber in Hollywood.

the islander

25 cents

Fashions • Homes • Beachcomber Issue 1948

DON THE BEACHCOMBER

After serving in World War II as a hospitality officer, Don decamped to Hawaii in 1948, opening a sprawling tropical village to attract the many tourists visiting the islands. As one of the developers of the new International Marketplace in Waikiki, Don created the romantic vision of Polynesia that tourists were expecting.

**LEFT:** Don brought his pet Tahitian cannibal carving with him to the islands.

**ABOVE:** Don the Beachcomber in Waikiki.

ALOHA NUI!

"THERE'S NOUGHT NO DOUBT,
SO MUCH THE SPIRIT CALMS
AS RUM AND TRUE RELIGION"
DON JUAN, CANTOZ -- STANZA 34

I, SUNAKORA, Queen of DON THE BEACHCOMBER by Royal Prerogative, send greetings and do hereby declare that

*Lionel J. Coffin*

having met the stringent qualifications of all good pleasure seeking Beachcombers, in accordance with our sacred traditions hereby acknowledged, and shall be universally recognized as a:

BEACHCOMBER (First Class)

* ❋ * ❋ * ❋ * ❋ * ❋ * ❋ * ❋ * ❋ * ❋ *

A BEACHCOMBER'S Creed

Our Number One Pre-Requisite:
Never stand when you can sit,
And if you can—lie down a bit.

Relax—no matter what you do
Enjoying life is up to you
The world is just a point of view.

When day is done—and comes the night
No pastime makes the stars so bright
As greeting dusk with Rum's Delight.

Of ALL Life's Pleasures deeply drink
At every worry give a wink,
It's MUCH MUCH later than you think.

DON THE BEACHCOMBER

After opening the first Beachcomber franchise in Chicago with his wife, Sunny Sund, the two decided to divide their enterprise between the continental U.S. and Hawaii with Don remaining an advisor to the mainland operations. In 1953, Sunny Sund brought the third Beachcomber outpost to Palm Springs.

CHOOSES PALM SPRINGS—Sunny Sunds, owner and operator of the famed Don The Beachcomber cafes in Hollywood and Chicago, chose Palm Springs as the site for her third venture. The noted spot will open in Sunset Towers in December.

Don the Beachcomber, Noted Cafe, Coming to the Village

**ABOVE CENTER:** The Palm Springs Don the Beachcomber was located in the center of the Village.

**FAR LEFT:** As Queen Sunakora, Sunny Sund gave Beachcomber certificates to loyal customers.

Don the Beachcomber in Chicago.

In the 1950s, the Cantonese food served at Don the Beachcomber was still new and exotic to many Americans. The delectable tidbits mixed well with the variety of tropical concoctions on the Beachcomber menu.

Confucius say: "For celebrations, No better brews than Don's libations."

DON THE BEACHCOMBER ®

1101 N. PALM CANYON DR.     PH. 325-2061

**LEFT:** Among Palm Springs glitterati frequenting the Beachcomber were mid-century modern tract developer Robert Alexander (center) next to his glamorous wife, Helene, with friends.

# DON THE BEACHCOMBER

**DR. FUNK**
For instant health

**ZOMBIE**
Created at Don the Beachcomber, Hollywood in 1934. Its crowning touch, a tot of the rich rum known as Demerara

**MISSIONARY'S DOWNFALL**
Fresh, crushed mint leaves give this temptress her lovely color

**PI YI**
As Hawaiian as "Aloha", including fresh crushed pineapple straight from the Islands

**TAHITIAN RUM PUNCH**
South Seas Magic in a glass

**VICIOUS VIRGIN**
Divinely light Puerto Rican and noble Old St. Croix rums go into this delicacy

**DON'S PEARL**
A perfect jewel, combining Passion Fruit, Puerto Rican Light Rum and a few secrets

**PEARL DIVER**
Full of bubbles, big and lustrous as those shining gems

**SHARK'S TOOTH**
A toothsome drink with a bit of a bite

**THREE DOTS & A DASH**
...-V
An heroic drink that includes the very special rum, *Martinique*

**PLANTER'S RUM PUNCH**
Honorable Ancestor to the mixed rum drink

**DAIQUIRI**
The drink that put the Caribbean on the map

**RUM JULEP**
An old favorite sparked with Paminto O Dram, a most sophisticated rum liqueur

**COFFEE GROG**
The perfect capper to a Beachcomber dinner

**MYSTERY GARDENIA**
Something new in floral arrangements
A change-of-taste mixture

**DON BEACH**
His favorite drink, named for "Himself"

**BEACHCOMBER'S GOLD**
A priceless concoction with just enough absinthe to make the heart grow fonder

**DEMERARA DRY FLOAT**
A hearty whistle wetter

**NEVER SAY DIE**
Or, if you must, have one for the road

**TEST PILOT**
One of the better ways to fly!

**NAVY GROG**
Powerfully good, laced with stout-hearted Hudson Bay 91.4...a rum to remember

**COBRA'S FANG**
Had it been the serpent in the Garden of Eden, man's history might be jollier

**Q.B. COOLER**
Jamaican Dark Rum, Herbsaint, Ginger...a few of the exotic ingredients in this quite different drink

**BEACHCOMBER'S PUNCH**
Don's inspired version of an old favorite

## AT THE BEACHCOMBER'S
# The Stars Earn Their Chopsticks

**By DOUG BROWN**

Stars and celebrities and the Hollywood set may come to the desert, stay, and then leave. But at one place in town they always stay, season-round.

chief beachcomber Ray Fine, president of the Beachcomber Corporation. "Yes, the chopsticks really denote the customer's loyalty."

There are many loyal beach-

the recipes, and the bartender the drink concoctions. The drink titles raise many an eyebrow, and when tasted can do the same, yet pleasingly!

The original Beachcomber

tion is a family one. This is a big family.

The man at the helm has been a restaurant man for years, except for service in both Pacific and European theaters

However, there are many, many "beachcombers," both from all walks of life, from the world of show business, stage, screen, all entertainment media, and John Q. Public. And the

The Palm Springs Don the Beachcomber continued the celebrity clientele tradition of the Hollywood original. Prominent desert vacationers like Frank Sinatra and Joan Crawford who frequented the Hollywood Beachcomber found themselves at home at the Palm Springs location.

**ABOVE:** A sampling of the Palm Springs area celebrity homes.

**FAR LEFT:** Movie star Joan Crawford and restaurant manager Ray Fine next to a display of Don the Beachcomber products.

**LEFT:** Two happy customers in front of the chopstick cabinet.

**BELOW:** Actors Robert Wagner and wife Natalie Wood with friends and chopsticks.

RENOWNED
CANTONESE FOOD
IN AN ATMOSPHERE
OF THE SOUTH SEAS

DON the BEACHCOMBER

OPEN DAILY FROM 5 P.M. • 120 VIA LOLA • FOR RESERVATIONS PHONE 2061

PALM SPRINGS

The tradition of awarding devoted customers their own personal set of chopsticks in an engraved bamboo tube was brought from the Hollywood spot to Palm Springs.

# Don the Beachcomber

## PALM SPRINGS, CALIF.

The seasonal opening of Don the Beachcomber Palm Springs was a community enterprise, a society bash, and a Hollywood preview all in one. Genial host Roy "Brad" Bradley was master of ceremonies over a joyful crowd of revelers imbibing Don's formidable potions.

**NEAR RIGHT:** Host Roy Bradley spreading aloha.

**RIGHT AND OPPOSITE:** Various photos of jovial Don the Beachcomber guests in Palm Springs.

# Rum and True Religion

### By DAVE SWANEY

WHAT MORE CAN be said of Don the Beachcomber? That it's a Palm Springs institution?; that it's the gathering place of desert society?; the place to be seen?; that it's the most atmospheric in town? Feh!

The simple truth, with no further embellishment, is simply that Don the Beachcomber is THE restaurant in Palm Springs. Of the three acknowledged top restaurants in the town, Don the Beachcomber is flagship.

No place is further in.

In 1961, Sunny Sund partnered with a group of investors led by Barron Hilton to enlarge the Palm Springs location. Clif and Lou Sawyer were responsible for the redecoration and Ray Fine became general manager. Soon, the Beachcomber group expanded to other locations with the Beachcomber character taking on a more youthful appearance.

**ABOVE:** Clif Sawyer's 1962 rendering for the expanded Palm Springs Beachcomber.

**NEAR RIGHT:** The now rare Don the Beachcomber mug.

**FAR RIGHT:** A Beachcomber matchbook advertising several locations.

DON THE BEACHCOMBER®
HOST TO DIPLOMAT AND BEACHCOMBER, PRINCE AND PIRATE

ISLAND OF MAHUUKONA WHERE GOOD RUM IS IMMORTALIZED AND DRINKING IS AN ART

Don the BEACHCOMBER ®

HOLLYWOOD, CALIF.
1727 No. McCADDEN PL.

PALM SPRINGS, CALIF.
1101 No. PALM CANYON DR.

ST. PAUL, MINNESOTA
HILTON HOTEL

CHICAGO, ILLINOIS
101 EAST WALTON PL.

LAS VEGAS, NEVADA
HOTEL SAHARA

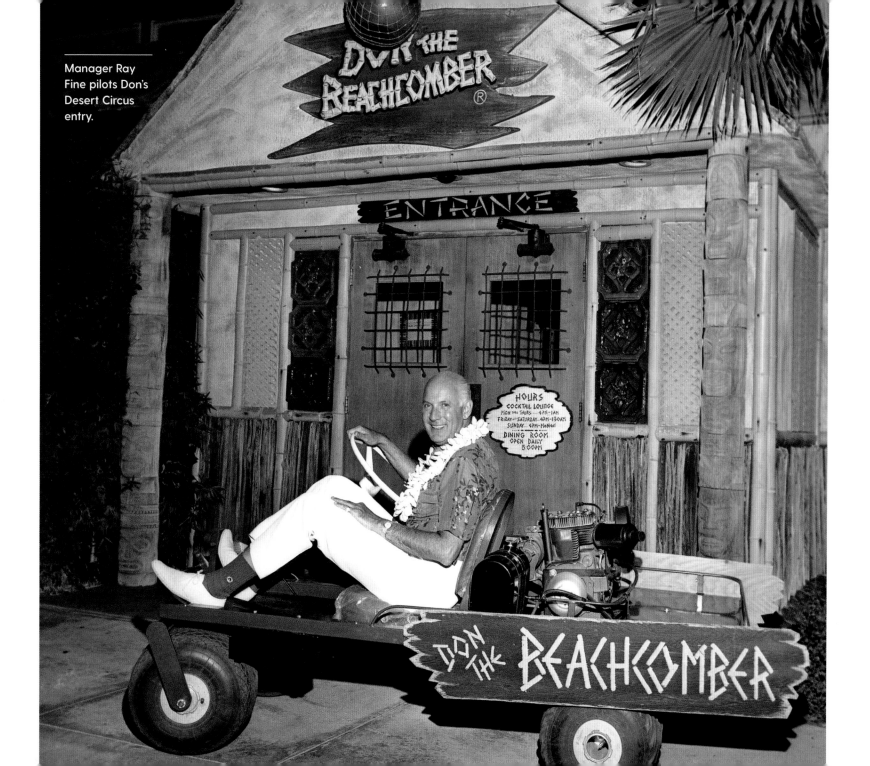

Manager Ray Fine pilots Don's Desert Circus entry.

# 8

# IDOLS *and* A-FRAMES

**TROPICANA**

FRESNO, CALIFORNIA

**B**y the mid-1950s, a new player appeared on the stage of Polynesia Americana. Uniting modernism and primitivism, the Polynesian idol commonly referred to as the Tiki became the ambassador of the "Island" lifestyle.

When, in the late 1950s, the demand for Tiki statues outstripped the supply from the islands, American artists were hired to create Tikis inspired by Oceanic Art books and other available sources. The results were a new fusion of authentic Polynesian art with modernist and cartoony influences. Ultimately these hybrids became restaurant logos on menus, matchbooks, ashtrays, and decorative statues, creating a uniquely American Pop art genre.

**TOP RIGHT:** The California-based architectural firm of Armet and Davis, famous for perfecting the Googie architectural style, designed the Hale Tiki restaurant in Philadelphia. It was an early concept for what became the Kona Kai, the flagship of Marriott's Kona Kai chain.

**BOTTOM RIGHT:** Various uses of logo Tikis.

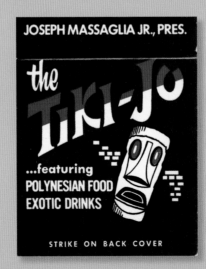

JOSEPH MASSAGLIA JR., PRES.

the TIKI-JO

...featuring
POLYNESIAN FOOD
EXOTIC DRINKS

STRIKE ON BACK COVER

EAST WING

OPENING JUNE 17th

Ren Clark's
Polynesian Village

Exotic Food and Drink

Three Beautiful Dining Rooms and Cocktail Lounge

**ABOVE LEFT:** The interior of Ren Clark's Polynesian Village in Fort Worth, Texas.

**ABOVE:** Trader Vic's went modern with the logo Tiki and A-frame concept.

**BOTTOM LEFT:** Diners found themselves supping under the gaze of pagan idols.

As the premier date growing region in the United States, the Coachella Valley was fertile ground for the raw material used by Tiki carvers—the palm tree.

Sun-Gold Date Gardens. · · LARGEST IN AMERICA
DISTINCTIVE GUEST RANCH IN CONNECTION

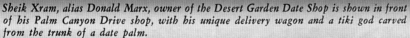

*Sheik Xram, alias Donald Marx, owner of the Desert Garden Date Shop is shown in front of his Palm Canyon Drive shop, with his unique delivery wagon and a tiki god carved from the trunk of a date palm.*

**ABOVE TOP:** An early example of a date farm tourist stop.

**ABOVE:** Two palm tree trunk Tikis at the Oasis Date Garden shop near Indio.

**OPPOSITE:** The Desert Garden Date Farm gift shop with the owner's wife proudly presenting the fruits of their harvest surrounded by primitive palm tree art.

Over time, roadside date stands evolved into expansive gift and souvenir shops where Tikis were sold alongside other merchandise.

Together with the image of the Tiki, the word "Tiki" gained popularity as a label for businesses promising the ambiance of the Polynesian islands in the desert.

**INSET LEFT:** Tiki Sands apartments in Rancho Mirage.

**INSET RIGHT:** Tiki Gardens apartments in Palm Desert.

**LEFT:** Hotel Tiki Palms on North Palm Canyon Drive.

**ABOVE:** Tiki Jojo motel apartments in Cathedral City.

In 1966, so-called Tiki Girls sold colorful plastic leis to benefit the inaugural Hawaiian Festival Week in Palm Springs. As part of the event, a Tiki torch parade required the replacement of 300 parking meter heads with flaming Tiki torches.

**ABOVE:** Dressed in fitted muumuus, jubilant Tiki Girls were the official greeters of Hawaiian Festival Week.

**TIKI TIME**—Preparing for Friday's Tiki Torch Parade are Tiki girl Martha Steed and Virginia (Jinks) Caddes, Palm Springs Meter maid. The girls are dem- onstrating how parking meter heads will be removed to insert tiki torches to line Palm Canyon Drive for the parade. Parking meter heads come off Friday.

# The Pele *(Pay-lay)* an all-aluminum car

The Pele is a Kaiser Aluminum design that incorporates today's practical, proved developments in aluminum automotive usage. Trim and transmission, bumpers and body, doors and differential—*all aluminum!*

And you may be certain that you will be building cars like the Pele, or components suggested in its design. Every year, more and more aluminum is being designed into American automobiles.

**Ravenswood** – source of highest quality aluminum

Ravenswood, West Virginia, is the location of what is perhaps the most *quality-minded* aluminum plant anywhere—the new Kaiser Aluminum reduction plant and rolling mill. Both by location and by layout, this plant is ideally situated to supply you the highest-quality aluminum available today.

Ask us, if you like, this question:

**"What Is The Difference In Aluminum From Ravenswood?"** (and please turn to back page)

KAISER ALUMINUM

In the 1950s, jet design influenced modern stylists and architects. Cars and buildings took on the shape of rockets poised to blast off into space. The soaring gables of A-frames became a favorite architectural design applied to homes, hotels, churches, fast food chains, bowling centers, and other structures.

**ABOVE:** The 1959 Lockheed Space Ferry.

**TOP RIGHT:** Late '50s car design epitomized the jet age.

**BOTTOM RIGHT:** Futurist lodgings at The Inn of Bermuda Dunes east of Palm Springs.

**TOP LEFT:** Modern churches reached for the heavens.

**TOP RIGHT:** An A-frame fireplace.

**LEFT:** Arizona A-frame dwelling.

**ABOVE:** Local architect Hugh Kaptur combined modernism with primitivism in this striking rendering of his Panorama Apartments design.

As it happened, original Pacific Island structures often took the form of A-frames and thus easily lent themselves to modern Polynesian Pop designs for restaurants, motels, and apartment buildings. Together with the Tiki, the A-frame became the signifier of Tiki modernism.

**TOP RIGHT:** Native village on the Caroline Islands, Micronesia.

**BOTTOM RIGHT:** Trader Vic's Scottsdale, Arizona.

**OPPOSITE:** Entrance to the Wonder Lodge hotel in Bakersfield, California.

**OPPOSITE TOP RIGHT:** Detail of the Maui Palms Apartments in Palm Desert.

**OPPOSITE BOTTOM RIGHT:** Hawaiian Village Apartments in Norwalk, California.

The Alexander Construction Company was one of the most prolific post-war residential builders in Palm Springs. The A-frame homes that architect Charles DuBois designed for the company won a certificate of merit from the National Association of Homebuilders. As the sales manager of the Alexander Construction Company, former Hawaii resident "Aloha Bob" Paine presented leis to the happy new owners of these Alexander abodes.

**ABOVE:** A classic Polynesian-style Alexander A-frame. Incorrectly dubbed "Swiss Miss" in the 1990s rediscovery of Palm Springs. The moniker unfortunately stuck by being perpetuated via the internet.

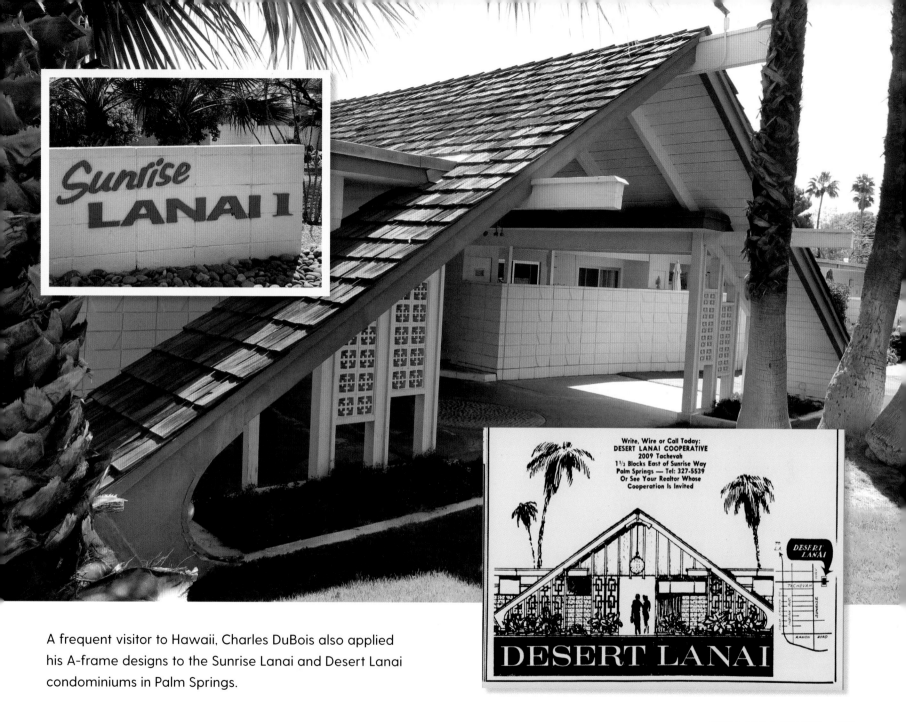

Sunrise
LANAI I

Write, Wire or Call Today:
DESERT LANAI COOPERATIVE
2009 Tachevah
1½ Blocks East of Sunrise Way
Palm Springs — Tel: 327-5539
Or See Your Realtor Whose
Cooperation Is Invited

DESERT LANAI

A frequent visitor to Hawaii, Charles DuBois also applied his A-frame designs to the Sunrise Lanai and Desert Lanai condominiums in Palm Springs.

ROYAL HAWAIIAN Estates . . . An exciting new concept in gracious desert living . . . a blending of the enchantment of the islands with the magic of sun-drenched desert life.

ROYAL HAWAIIAN ESTATES
is a group of 40 individual homes situated in Palm Springs' prestige location, South Palm Canyon Drive . . . minutes from world-famous country clubs, shops, clubs and restaurants . . . yet secluded and affording unique privacy in every way . . . Club-size swimming pools, putting greens, poolside cabanas, Gold Medallion electric living, sunken breeze-free recreational areas and private carports, are but a few of the features in Palm Springs' most exciting and luxurious new development. ROYAL HAWAIIAN Estates affords complete residential privacy . . . maintainance-free . . manager service . . landscaped luxury . . all this and more can be yours when you reside at Palm Springs' finest — ROYAL HAWAIIAN ESTATES

The Royal Hawaiian Estates condominiums designed by local architect Richard "Rick" Harrison were the most expressionistic application of jet age modernism to a housing development in Palm Springs. With its jutting patio dividers and geometric outrigger embellishments, the Royal Hawaiian remains a unique example of Tiki Modern. The complex was designated a Palm Springs Historic District in 2010.

**LEFT:** Royal Hawaiian Estates opened in 1961.

Here's the Jet Age *on wheels!* Aerodynamic Plymouth '56

Mirroring the jet age design of 1950s American cars, the Royal Hawaiian is the only development in Palm Springs bearing tailfins.

THE Cal Tjader TRIO

THREE LITTLE WORDS
CHARLEY'S QUOTE
IVY
LULLABY OF THE LEAVES
THESE FOOLISH THINGS
GIVE ME THE SIMPLE LIFE
VIBRA-THARPE
CHOPSTICKS - MAMBO

fantasy
3-9

**ABOVE:** This Cal Tjader LP cover is a fine example of mid-century modern expressionism.

Mid-century modern architects like Rick Harrison took their inspiration from the great innovators of twentieth-century architecture such as Frank Lloyd Wright.

**BOTTOM LEFT:** Frank Lloyd Wright's Taliesen West compound in Scottsdale, Arizona.

**BELOW:** "Shin'en Kan" Residence of 1956 by architect Bruce Goff in Oklahoma.

Today the Royal Hawaiian condos are inhabited by mid-century modern aficionados and Tiki enthusiasts. A few of the original Easter Island head Tikis remain poolside. Unfortunately, the two six-foot-tall palm tree Tikis that initially guarded the entrance were stolen in September 1961 and never replaced.

*Exotic plantings and an attractive young lady (Sherry Wager) for Royal Hawaiian Estates.*

# ✦ 9 ✦

# TIKI MOTOR HOTELS
## *in the* DESERT

The American motel experienced an unprecedented boom during the 1950s and 1960s. The convenience and ease of parking your land yacht right in front of your room appealed to a new generation of motorists. Paralleling the rise of the Polynesian theme, roadside motels became Tiki islands.

tropics hotel
411 E. PALM CANYON DR.
PALM SPRINGS, CALIFORNIA

Southern California developer Ken Kimes benefited from the motel craze by building increasingly more elaborate motor hotels in the region. The Palm Springs location was his thirty-seventh operation, with five of them being Tropics Hotels in the Tiki style concept.

---

**BOTTOM LEFT:** Ken Kimes used a Rip Van Winkle cartoon character at all of his motor hotels.

The impressive A-frame of the Tropics was intended to capture the attention of motorists, fulfilling the architectural concept of building-as-sign. Its upward sweeping form mirrored the Papua New Guinea meeting houses in Melanesia.

**LEFT:** The Tropics' A-frame porte cochere.

**INSET:** Men's Meeting House on Muschu Island, North New Guinea.

Besides its A-frame, other eye-catching features of the Tropics were its tall Tikis with root-ball hairdos and its original sign in the form of a Polynesian outrigger canoe. An on-site Waltah Clarke Tropics shop offering Hawaiian fashions completed the island resort flair.

TELEPHONE 327-1391

KEN KIMES BUILT MOTOR HOTELS

Tropics HOTEL RESTAURANT

tropics hotel

RESTAURANT AND COCKTAIL LOUNGE

411 E.PALM CANYON DR.,PALM SPRINGS,CALIF.

CLOSE COVER BEFORE STRIKING

**LEFT:** A Tiki with a root-ball hairdo towers over this Tropics Hotel guest.

**ABOVE:** Early Tropics matchbook depicting the outrigger.

**OPPOSITE:** The baroque mid-century splendor of the Palm Springs Tropics.

The young sculptor Ed Crissman was the artistic genius behind the more than twenty Tiki statues populating the Palm Springs Tropics grounds.

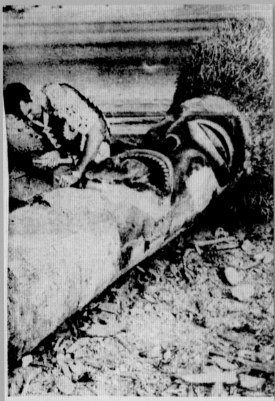

**ARTIST** Ed Crissman puts the finishing touches on one of the many large tiki figures surrounding the Tropics Hotel. This 18-foot length of palm tree is inverted so the roots become the hair for the Polynesian character. Crissman created more than 20 of the original South Seas carvings for the decor of the lavish new hotel.

**ABOVE:** A rare example of a copper plaque crediting the artist.

Ed Crissman worked with Oceanic Arts in Whittier, California, a major supplier of Polynesian décor and building materials. Co-owner Leroy Schmaltz carved all of the signage and Tiki details for the hotel's Reef Bar (previously the Congo Room).

**LEFT:** Entrance to the Reef Bar (Congo Room).

**ABOVE:** A unique example of Leroy Schmaltz's artistry was the saloon swinging doors carved with Tiki faces.

The original 1963 Congo Room steak house was a bizarre mixture of African, Moroccan Regency, and coffee shop modern décor.

**BOTTOM LEFT:** The Tropics pool and Tiki statue visible from the window illustrate the odd contrast of themes.

**BOTTOM RIGHT:** Standing outside the Congo Room this statue was based on the art of the Hemba people of Eastern Luba, Congo, as interpreted by sculptor Jo De Trapani.

A subterranean cocktail lounge called The Cellar featured live entertainment and a collection of wines under a faux grotto ceiling. Particularly unusual was the fact that cellars in Palm Springs were exceptionally rare. Eventually this cave filled with water and was encased in concrete.

Although other Tiki themed motels existed in Southern California, only the Tropics motel chain featured five locations in that style. All were decorated with Tiki statuary carved by Ed Crissman.

Like several of the other Tropics hotels, the Blythe location included a Sambo's pancake house.

tropics hotel LOCATIONS

LOS ANGELES
ANAHEIM
PALM SPRINGS SAMBOS
INDIO
BLYTHE SAMBOS

TROPICS INDIO
TROPICS BLYTHE
MECCA MOTEL DISNEYLAND

Blythe, California
tropics
MOTOR HOTEL

THE BEST
Western MOTELS

Tropics MOTOR HOTEL

RELAX IN STYLE
COCKTAILS
SWIM

SAMBO'S
PANCAKES

Another desert town in the Coachella Valley that was home to a Tropics Motor Hotel was Indio. Its original neon sign still beckons the weary traveler today.

The Modesto Tropics contained its own freestanding A-frame Tiki cocktail lounge as well as a Sambo's restaurant.

**LEFT:** Consistent with the elaborate motel signs appearing throughout the country, some of the Tropics presented this soaring modernist roadside beacon.

CLOSE COVER BEFORE STRIKING

**TOP LEFT:** Although the titular character of Sambo's restaurants was a West Indian boy, by the 1970s the term had degraded into a racial slur and was slowly removed from its advertising.

**LEFT:** By the 1990s, this giant Ed Crissman Tiki required a supportive headband to keep it erect.

Built near the Palm Springs Tropics in 1964, the Tiki Spa was a modest mom-and-pop apartment hotel offering a sauna, swimming pool, and hot pools.

The Tiki Spa featured A-frames with outrigger beams and ubiquitous Tiki statuary.

**ABOVE LEFT:** The now-vanished Tiki Spa sign in 1992.

# ALOHA JHOE'S—
## A Tiki Gesamtkunstwerk

The German term "Gesamtkunstwerk" denotes a "total work of art." Aloha Jhoe's represents such a synthesis of the arts within the genre of Tiki modernism. The group of people who came together to design this phantasmagoria were all mid-century masters of their craft.

**OPPOSITE:** Clockwise from bottom left: restaurateur Milton F. Kreis, general manager Lew Levy, architect William Cody, and designer John De Cuir proudly display their project.

**RIGHT:** The logo Tiki "Aloha Jhoe" on the matchcover.

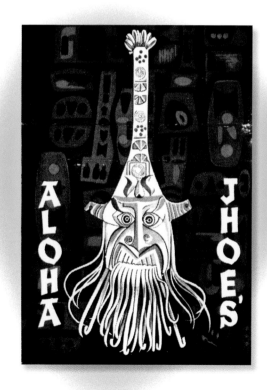

Before the advent of Aloha Jhoe's there was The Springs, perhaps the most architecturally expressive restaurant ever designed in the desert. Designed by local architect William Cody in 1957, the building was a symphony of angles hovering over desert landscaping—a sculptural masterpiece of wood, rock, glass, and metal. Four years later, the north portion of the structure was transformed into a Polynesian paradise. Still, the spirit of The Springs would permeate Aloha Jhoe's.

**BELOW AND BOTTOM RIGHT:** The expressionist angles of The Springs.

**UPPER RIGHT:** The building's namesake spring welled up behind the glass and rock wall near the main entrance.

NOW OPEN! *Palm Springs'-- and the world's-- most exotic new restaurant:* THE SPRINGS *in Cameron Center*

.... corner of the Villa Nova Room where a spring wells up behind the glass and rock wall.

THE SPRINGS

RESTAURANT ● COFFEE SHOP ● COCKTAIL BAR
YOUR HOST: . . . . . . . . . ALLEN DALE
960 SOUTH PALM CANYON DRIVE
TELEPHONE 9692 FOR RESERVATIONS

Eminent architectural historian and author Alan Hess considers The Springs by William Cody to be the most sophisticated example of Googie Modern ever constructed in America. "Cody understood the architectural potential of Googie's geometries, integral art, and roadside presence to appeal to a wide audience."

**ABOVE:** The modernist lines of the fireplace reflect the avant-garde design of The Springs.

**RIGHT:** Famed California muralist Millard Sheets was commissioned to create a wall of traditional Navajo designs.

A modernist Tiki oasis rising out of the desert, Aloha Jhoe's featured an eye-catching cornucopia of Oceanic art. The restaurant invited you to "be a Polynesian Potentate" and "say aloha to your friends at the romantic Royal Tiki bar."

George E. Cameron, Jr.
"Building For Tomorrow"
Palm Springs, California

• George E. Cameron, Jr. Oil Co.
• Desert Sun
• K O E S  AM · FM
• Cameron Center
• George E. Cameron, Jr. Enterprises

MEET US AT

KUE SUEY LEE – Head Chef
DIMINGO MANGENTE
Bar Manager
MILTON KREIS – Owner

ALOHA JHOE'S

Open daily and Sundays at 5 p.m.
Continuous entertainment in the Royal Tiki Bar
For Reservations: Phone 324-8941

CLASSIC CANTONESE CUISINE

Watch for the torch-lit
god ALOHA JHOE at
950 S. PALM CANYON DRIVE

CAMERON CENTER
ALOHA JHOES
WOOLWORTHS
MAYFAIR MARKET
JEFFREY'S

The logo Tiki "Aloha Jhoe" was a giant version of ceremonial dance masks from Papua New Guinea. At night a gas torch blazed from the tip of the Tiki's topknot.

**FAR LEFT:** Palm Springs mayor Frank Bogert (center) with his daughter and restaurant owner Milton F. Kreis.

Movie production designers Lyle Wheeler and John De Cuir were the principal artists commissioned to provide the look of Aloha Jhoe's. Their participation confirms the long-standing connection between Hollywood set designers and Polynesian Pop.

**LEFT:** John De Cuir (left) and Lyle Wheeler with De Cuir's rendering for the set of *Cleopatra*.

**ABOVE TOP:** De Cuir's work for the 1954 film *Carmen Jones*.

**ABOVE:** A painted island backdrop on a studio soundstage.

the art direction

lyle wheeler and john de cuir

Wheeler and De Cuir were the art directors for the movie version of the hit musical *South Pacific*, which was reflected in their work for Aloha Jhoe's.

**BOTTOM RIGHT:** Closeup of John De Cuir's initial rendering of Aloha Jhoe's entrance.

RODGERS AND HAMMERSTEIN'S SOUTH PACIFIC

**FINISHING TOUCH** is applied to face on totem pole by Jim Casey. Casey is former musician, orchestra leader and television director. He started woodcarving while serving in Navy during World War II.

Sculptor Jim Casey was responsible for the elaborate totem pole signposts and the variety of carvings for the exterior of Aloha Jhoe's. Casey's Tikis also graced the tropical Mystery Island on the Pacific Ocean Park pier in Santa Monica and the Luau restaurant in Beverly Hills.

The giant tropical bird design was based on Papua New Guinea meeting house gable figures and also appeared at other American Tiki temples.

---

**INSET:** The Kona Kai restaurant entrance at the Philadelphia Marriott Hotel features a bird gable figure.

**LEFT:** A spirit bird carving on top of a soaring Haus Tambaran in Papua New Guinea.

Another mid-century artist associated with Aloha Jhoe's was the prolific ceramicist Sascha Brastoff. A perforated candleholder from his line was used to decorate the Aloha Jhoe's tables.

**Sascha Brastoff**

Designer extraordinary—a modern Cellini—creator
of contemporary home accessories of breathtaking beauty and
functional worth. Already recognized internationally for
his fabulous signed ceramic originals and hand made dinnerware, he
now presents a collection of custom made table lamps...
a series of original paintings on ceramic panels...and, proudest
achievement of all, his new fine china tableware in exquisite
translucent porcelain, each piece a genuine work of art.
Look for the signature in America's most discriminating stores.

Sascha Brastoff Products, Inc.

Studios: West Los Angeles 64, California

**OPPOSITE:** Mayor Frank Bogert and his wife, Janice, being served the communal Orchid Bowl cocktail.

**BELOW:** A unique lacquered bamboo coffee mug.

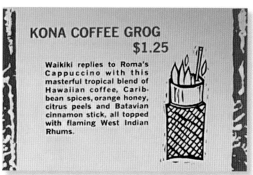

**KONA COFFEE GROG**
**$1.25**

Waikiki replies to Roma's
Cappuccino with this
masterful tropical blend of
Hawaiian coffee, Carib-
bean spices, orange honey,
citrus peels and Batavian
cinnamon stick, all topped
with flaming West Indian
Rhums.

**ABOVE:** Two young moderns under the spell of Aloha Jhoe, *Polynesian God of Food and Drink*, designed by Lyle Wheeler and built by Jim Casey over The Springs modernist fireplace.

**OPPOSITE:** The whimsical drink descriptions in the Aloha Jhoe's cocktail menu are a classic example of Polynesian Pop poetry.

## ALOHA JHOES

Rhum, the historic drink of hearty buccaneers who sailed under the Jolly Roger, holds the key to the treasure chest of pleasure. Exotic in taste and thirst-quenching in effect, Rhum helps to fulfill the modern need of relaxation.

The Rhum cellar of Aloha Jhoe's is stocked with the finest blends of this nectar. No better selection of Rhum is to be found anywhere in the world. Our mixologists are equal to the task of blending hundreds of Rhum drinks that will thrill your palate, satisfy your thirst and set you in the proper mood to enjoy Cantonese cuisine at its best. May we suggest that you consult our food menu and try some appetizers— they highly complement these fine Rhum drinks.

MAUNA LOA ... 1.00

WEST INDIAN PUNCH 1.10

GREEN DRAGON 1.10

DESIRE ... 1.10

BLONDE WITCH 1.70

IWALANI ... .95

MAUI COOLER, limit 3 ... 1.70

### ALOHA JHOE'S ORCHID BOWL (4 Persons) ... $4.00

Despite what you may have heard to the contrary—this is positively the grand-daddy of all bowl games. It takes four winners to play and when you do, every day magically becomes New Years. Ask our equipment manager—he's also your waiter—to suit your team up and then you're on your own, sipping delightfully down a field wet with fine varieties of the world's finest rhum. You'll savor the Caribbean spices, the fine lime and the passion fruit juices as you pass the yard marker on the way to a score.

### COBRA'S FANG, $1.25

The mellow effect of this 151 proof Demerara Rhum, Falernum and tropical fruit juices will excite and delight your taste buds.

### ACE PILOT (limit 2) $1.90

As a precaution for your well-being and safety, we've put a ceiling of two on this. After all, it's serious putting a man into orbit.

Virgin Island Rhums, passion fruit and Jhoe's original blend of mixes.

### ALOHA MAIDEN $ .95

Aloha Maiden, not in the sense of a goodbye but rather in the sense of hello to love. You'll both know that you've just arrived in a new kind of paradise, drinking a splendid blend of Trinidad Rhum, Green Allspice Liqueur, Orange Blossom Honey, Angostura Bitters and tropical limes.

MOONKIST PINEAPPLE 2.00

CUBAN DAIQUIRI .95

GARDENIA COCKTAIL 1.00

BORA BORA DRY FLOAT ... 1.10

ZOMBIE, limit 2, .. 2.00

JAMAICA PLANTERS ... 1.10

COCONUT RHUM 2.00

TAHITIAN RHUM PUNCH ... $1.00

Mr. Christian and Captain Bligh could have peacefully settled their "Mutiny on the Bounty" if they had feasted with this delightful drink. Tropical passion fruits exotically blended with The Islands greenest limes and old island Rhums will make your Captain Bligh bearable.

### NAVY GROG $1.70

You'll acquire the sea-legs of a salty sailor without ever boarding a ship, if you exceed our limit of three to a customer on this drink. A Rhum punch as robust as the brave men of the U.S. Navy.

### SHARK'S TOOTH $1.10

A snubby variety of the notorious man-eater but none-the-less, deadly. Eighteen years of aging give this Jamaica Rhum Liqueur drink a mellow bite that you'll enjoy.

### V. J. DAY ... $1.10

You'll shout victoriously at your enemy's unconditional surrender, after two of these. Highly recommended for successful Summit Conferences. Rhum, HMS-style, Caribbean spices, Falernum and Angostura.

### DEEP SEA DIVER $1.10

Three fathoms of delicious West India Rhums, Falernum and a mysterious mixture of tropical fruit. Makes you qualify as a Scubba diver without getting wet.

KONA COFFEE GROG $1.25

Waikiki replies to Roma's Cappuccino with this masterful tropical blend of Hawaiian coffee, Caribbean maple honey, citrus peels and Batavian cinnamon stick, all topped with flaming West Indian Rhums.

### ALOHA JHOE'S PUNCH ... $1.20

The specialty of the house —and a secret that we're sworn to keep. It's the answer all for the esoteric person who seeks out the aesthetic.

### JAMAICA RHUM JULEP ... $1.10

A drink that could change the habits of a loyal Kentucky Colonel. We've kept the mint and added an ancient blend of mellow Rhum liquers ... the bouquet is exquisite ... the taste divine.

MAI TAI $1.85

If you can't say no, for goodness sake, say MAI TAI. The leisurely Hawaiian answer to a hurried Madison Avenue Martini. Fine old French Martinique and Jamaica Rhums slyly blended with exotic liqueurs and fragrant green limes.

### BUCCANEER'S GROG $ .95

Fifteen men on a dead man's chest—Heave ho my lads and lean into this hardy elixir of very old New England Rhums, stirred into Pimiento Dram, Trinidad Bitters and Maple Sugar.

### GOLD CUP $ .95

Hydro-plane pilots race all year for this. You'll feel like a winner after one sip and glide smoothly across the finish line. Fine Jamaica gold Rhums spliced to West India Liqueurs.

### ISLAND PEARL, $1.10

Jhoe's version of Green Stamps. You get a bonus of a genuine cultured pearl with every fifth drink. String along with this mixture of white Rhums, tropical fruit syrups and juicy limes and soon you'll have a necklace.

In addition to the exotic drinks listed above, Aloha Jhoe's prides itself on a complete selection of all fine imported and domestic distilled spirits. Our cocktails are prepared with loving care and our wine cellar is well stocked with world renowned prize winning vintages.

## JHOE'S ALL TIME FAVORITES

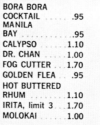 

| | | |
|---|---|---|
| BORA BORA COCKTAIL ... .95 | MONA MYER'S PUNCH ... 2.00 | TABOO ... 1.10 |
| MANILA BAY ... .95 | NEGRITA MILK PUNCH ... 1.00 | TONGAREVA ... 1.00 |
| CALYPSO ... 1.10 | NEGRITA RHUM COCKTAIL ... .95 | ZULU NO. 1 ... 1.60 |
| DR. CHAN ... 1.00 | PAGO PAGO ... 1.10 | ZULU NO. 2 ... .95 |
| FOG CUTTER ... 1.70 | RAROTONGA ... 1.10 | BARREL O' RHUM ... 2.25 |
| GOLDEN FLEA ... .95 | RHUM SWIZZLE ... 1.10 | HAWAIIAN PUNCH 1.10 |
| HOT BUTTERED RHUM ... 1.10 | SCORPION ... 1.70 | IMPATIENT VIRGIN .95 |
| IRITA, limit 3 ... 1.70 | SILVER CUP ... .95 | O. F. O. SWIZZLE 1.60 |
| MOLOKAI ... 1.00 | SKULL & BONES 1.10 | PANAMA DAIQUIRI .95 |
| | | SPECIAL DAIQUIRI 1.10 |
| | | SPECIAL PLANTERS 1.90 |
| | | TAWI TAWI, limit 3 1.70 |

A.F. RAIGOSA & ASSOCIATES
• LAKE DESIGNERS • LAND DEVELOPERS • BUILDERS
*Gardena, California*

...PLANNED PRIVATE LAKE DEVELOPMENT, WITH CUSTOM HOMESITES
...2500 FT. AIRCRAFT RUNWAY ... SAILING, GAME FISHING AND
WATER-SKIING ...THREE ENCHANTING "ESCAPE" ISLANDS
...DOCKING FACILITIES AND MARINA ...SWIM BEACH
...PUTTING GREEN ...HILLTOP WATERFALL & BROOK...

"Lake
NEWBERRY
DESIGNED BY
80 ACRES

# DEEP DESERT TIKI

T he desert has always attracted boosters, be they dreamers, visionaries, or speculators. The fantasy of a Polynesian paradise within one's reach appealed to the same pioneering mindset, leading to some astonishing flights of fancy.

---

**OPPOSITE:** Tahiti in the middle of the desert? Why not!

**ABOVE:** Imagination takes wing with the Lake Loreen *Tiki Bird*.

For two years starting in 1905, the Colorado River was accidentally diverted into a dry lakebed located at the far southeastern end of the Coachella Valley. This would become the landlocked, 318-square-mile Salton Sea, 240 feet below sea level. By the late 1950s, the Salton Sea was a popular destination for swimming, boating, fishing, and speculative land development schemes. Of the latter, two of the most ambitious were located on opposite sides of the sea, each anchored by modern new recreational facilities—North Shore Beach & Yacht Club and Salton Bay Yacht Club.

**ABOVE:** A popular sun bathing and water sports destination.

**RIGHT:** Salton Sea . . . an investor's dream. The yachting life for the middle class.

*A desert paradise on the Great Salton Sea*

# SALTON SEA VISTA
## . . . AN INVESTOR'S DREAM

Whether you are in the market for property on which to build a home . . . looking for income investment land . . . or trying to find a growing community for expansion of your business, Salton Sea Vista has the logical answer for you, and at a price that is attractive!

Salton Sea Vista will grow . . . and your investment will grow along with it. Perhaps you were born fifty years too late to catch the Gold Rush . . . the Uranium cache, Newport, Palm Springs, . . . or even Wilshire and La Brea! But there's no reason NOW for you to miss this opportunity . . . and it doesn't take a 'bundle' to do it.

*Salton Sea Vista* ESTATES INC.
8348 BEVERLY BLVD., LOS ANGELES 48, CALIF., WE 3-9587

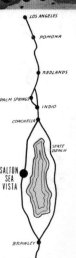

Salton Bay Yacht Club - Salton City. California
South of Palm Springs, between Indio and El Centro via Highway 99

MARINA
SALTON SEA BEACH

MARINA STORE
DRINKS, ICE, SNACKS
CAMPING
OPEN: 6 A.M.–EVERY DAY

**LEFT:** This way to the beach and marina.

**ABOVE:** Famed modernist architect Albert Frey designed the nautically inspired North Shore Yacht Club in 1958. Having fallen into ruin, it was fully restored in 2010.

Among the pioneering mavericks drawn to the Salton Sea was Helen Burns who settled on its west shores in 1949. Outgoing, energetic, and brimming with enthusiasm, she opened Helen's Beach House in the early 1950s, operating the widely known tropical restaurant, bar, and local hangout for three decades. Helen's numerous themed nights at the Beach House—especially her signature Hawaiian luau festivals—cemented Helen's reputation as Queen of the Salton Sea.

**TOP LEFT:** Helen Burns performing the hula at her Beach House.

**LEFT:** Luaus were extremely popular at the Salton Sea.

**ABOVE:** Helen's Beach House in the early 1960s.

Located not far from Helen's Beach House was the Salton Tiki bar/restaurant that opened in 1963, promising to serve lobster and steak with fine wines and champagne. It survived as a local watering hole until 1998.

**BELOW:** Summoning the American god of recreation to Salton Sea Beach.

The Salton Riviera Story...

*Picture of a Family Making Money*

Your dreams come true in...

SALTON RIVIERA

*California's fabulous new resort city on the Salton Sea*

Starting in the 1970s, a confluence of long-festering misfortunes reached critical mass. Initially, catastrophic flooding submerged many of the recreational facilities and dwellings along the shoreline. Then, high salinity from evaporation, and algae blooms from contaminated farm runoff, led to massive fish and avian die-offs. The resulting noxious odor marked the end of the Salton Sea as an investment opportunity and leisure destination.

**TOP LEFT:** Trailer Tiki culture at the Salton Sea's Bombay Beach.

**BOTTOM LEFT:** Abandoned trailers near the shore.

Intersection of Honolulu Way and Salton Bay Drive through an empty tract.

As dreams of desert development coincided with the fantasy of the mainland Polynesian paradise, people began to see South Seas chimeras in the badlands. With Gus Raigosa, it started innocently enough: He and his wife Loreen were looking for an affordable property outside of Los Angeles and ended up near Newberry Springs in the Mojave Desert. They found out that it was easy to tap into the groundwater and dug themselves a private lake. Soon friends got interested, and Gus saw an opportunity. He became a land developer.

"Lake Loreen"
NEWBERRY SPRINGS, CALIFORNIA
presents a fabulous new addition
Soon....

# CAMPERS JUNGLE
FEATURING OVER 400 SPACIOUS CAMPSITES
SURROUNDING "LAKE KALA-LAU" (the Wanderer)
SWIMMING, TENNIS, SHUFFLEBOARD, BAR-B-Q'S, LUAU'S,
FISHING, OUTRIGGERS, & FREE HULA LESSONS!!!

The Tiki island dream was nothing but democratic. Regardless of income and social standing, everyone could dream it. Gus Raigosa was a plumber at Lockheed Aircraft in Los Angeles, his wife a secretary there. With many of his friends being coworkers at Lockheed, the concept of "fly-in" resorts suggested itself. It had proven successful for the Desert Air in Rancho Mirage, why not a little further up north? A runway was graded, and the elaborately painted *Tiki Bird*, its interior outfitted in leopard print and shag carpet, flew eager guests and potential property buyers to Polynesia USA.

**LEFT:** All you need to create Polynesia in the desert.

**BELOW:** Come fly with me.

In the 1960s, concerns about drought, global warming, and possible land subsidence by depleting the aquifer were practically unknown. This was America and land was for the taking, and water, like oil in the 1920s, could be tapped on your own property just by digging a well. Drill a hole, leave a couple of dirt mounds, and you had a lake, complete with islands. The Raigosas built a lakeside model home, decorated it with black velvet paintings and red velvet furniture, and hired a couple of models to inhabit their South Sea storybook land.

For a while, the Polynesian Lake-of-Dreams that "Crazy" Gus had conjured up out of the arid land attracted visitors to its shallow shores to enjoy swimming, boating, fishing, and relaxing in beach lanais to the sounds of piped-in Hawaiian music.

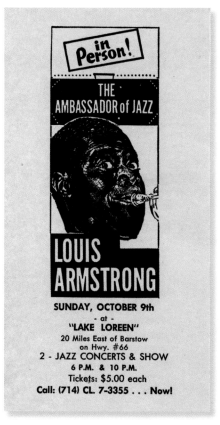

The Blue Lagoon restaurant offered "chicken of the Gods" and "exotically beautiful tropical drinks." Luaus promised "gigantic Polynesian warriors and beautiful Polynesian dancers" PLUS (obviously inspired by The Tikis in Monterey Park) a "huge gorilla act." On one memorable evening in 1966, Lake Loreen welcomed famed jazz veteran Louis Armstrong to its shores for two concerts.

Eventually, as the Tiki craze subsided, people got tired of making the trip to nowhere land, and the money to build the Raigosas' numerous lake paradises dried up. What remains there today are a few dusty roads with Hawaiian names surrounding a Lake Wainani, newspaper ads full of hyperbole, and most of all the artful renderings by Louis Nitti Jr. depicting desert lake communities dotted with A-frames and Tikis that never came into being. All are testament to the pervasiveness of the dream of Polynesia USA which could not possibly have been further removed from its origin than in the Mojave Desert.

Open from 1962 to 1977, El Tiki was a beloved neighborhood haunt for Imperial Valley residents from all walks of life. It was the brainchild of former elementary school teacher Ben Wilson who, bitten by the Tiki bug, picked up a chisel and started carving palms into Tikis. He then decided to open a Mexican restaurant just outside of El Centro, a mostly Hispanic community close to the Mexican border, and decorate it with his carvings. In his menu text, Ben explains: "One day while carving a Tiki, I noticed a definite resemblance to an Aztec god." He then proceeded to note that both Hawaii and Mexico are in the tropical zone, listing each country's similarities.

**BELOW:** The multicultural (American, Mexican, and Polynesian) El Tiki restaurant.

**BIGGEST GOD** — Ben Wilson of Wilson's Corner (his father bought the property in 1921) on Highway 111 examines a Tiki god he carved over a three-month period out of an old palm tree. The young-man-with-a-beard claims his is the largest Tiki god in California and describes it as a god of war.     (Staff Photo)

In the early 1960s Tiki, the Polynesian god of the artists, inspired many novice carvers to fashion their own version of this idol. El Tiki and its décor were exemplary for this American pop culture in two ways: First, in its self-made quality, conceived by someone with no art or restaurant experience; second, El Tiki exemplified the free-wheeling attitude toward mixing elements of different cultures to form a unique new style of exotic art.

**ABOVE:** A proud artist and his handiwork.

**ABOVE RIGHT:** The sign for the never-realized El Tikila franchise.

**RIGHT:** Having fun with cultural cliches.

# PALM SPRINGS TIKI TODAY

As Palm Springs has gained worldwide renown as a hub of mid-century modern architecture so has twentieth-century Polynesian Pop found a growing community of Tiki-style aficionados during the last twenty years. Both design genres originally coincided during the same time period in the 1950s, feeding off each other as opposite sides of the aesthetic spectrum. In today's Palm Springs they have come together again as a celebratory lifestyle.

**OPPOSITE:** Tiki torches flicker anew at the Caliente Tropics Hotel, illuminating one of the original 1963 Ed Crissman Tikis.

**RIGHT:** Happy Tiki revelers under the Tropics A-frame at the Tiki Caliente weekender.

Beginning in 2001, *Tiki News* fanzine editor Otto von Stroheim organized a gathering of Tiki enthusiasts from Los Angeles and the rest of California at the Caliente Tropics Motel in Palm Springs. Named Tiki Oasis, it blossomed into the largest Tiki festival in the country, attracting Tiki fans from all over the world.

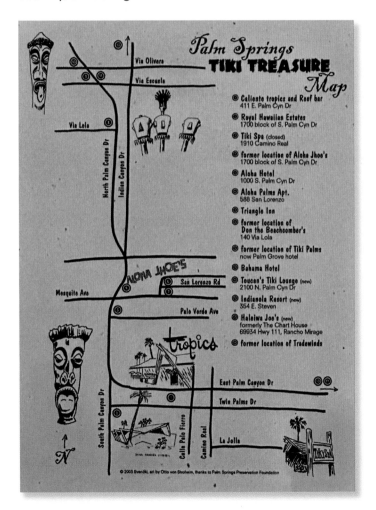

**LEFT:** By 2003, Tiki archaeologists had identified all the remaining vestiges of Palm Springs Polynesia and printed a treasure map for Tiki Oasis attendees.

**TOP ABOVE:** Tiki Oasis flyer, by Derek.

**ABOVE:** A group of early Tikiphiles gathered around a vintage Tiki at the Tropics.

The re-appreciation of mid-century modernism went hand in hand with the discovery of Tiki style as a unique facet of American pop culture. The Jetsons met the Flintstones as graphic artists and animators expressed their fondness for the two genres in colorful artworks depicting an eye-candy world of modern primitives at play.

**TOP LEFT:** Flyer for Tiki artists group show at M-Modern Gallery, by Chris Reccardi.

**TOP RIGHT:** This poster ushered in the age of Shag as the premier Palm Springs artist.

**LEFT:** A mid-century modern home with Tiki accents, by El Gato Gomez.

In 2001, an intended "upgrading" of the Tropics Motel into the prevailing generic Mediterranean style was averted by Palm Springs preservationist Peter Moruzzi when he presented Sven Kirsten's just-published *Book of Tiki* to the new owners, convincing them to keep the Tiki theme intact. When Tiki Oasis expanded to San Diego and Scottsdale, Reef Bar owner Rory Snyder took over the reins creating the Tiki Caliente weekender at the hotel. With the Reef as his successful headquarters, Snyder expanded his empire to include Le Fern cocktail bar and Mexican restaurant Sancho's (a nod to the Sambo's restaurant that originally occupied the space).

**LEFT AND BOTTOM RIGHT:** Reef Bar and Tiki Caliente posters, by Doug Horne.

**ABOVE:** Tiki impresario Rory Snyder in his element.

**TOP RIGHT:** Contemporary carving, by Bosko.

**ABOVE LEFT:** Sculptor John Mulder created a highly collectible series of Tiki mugs for the Reef and Tiki Caliente.

**ABOVE RIGHT:** An Ed Crissman Tiki made into a mug.

**BELOW:** Shenanigans at Tiki Caliente.

Comparing the 1966 Desert Sun dining guide to today's Palm Springs scene shows that some of the town's Tiki venues have miraculously survived. Though the subterranean Cellar at the Tropics has been entombed in concrete, one still has a choice of three exotic bar/restaurants in one location now, while the Bootlegger Tiki cocktail bar has breathed new life into the long-shuttered Don the Beachcomber building.

**ABOVE:** A Don The Beachcomber classic, the potent Demerara Dry Float, at Bootlegger Tiki.

**ABOVE RIGHT:** The shuttered Don The Beachcomber in the 1990s.

**RIGHT:** Bootlegger Tiki today in the original Don the Beachcomber building.

The Tonga Hut came to Palm Springs from its original 1958 location in North Hollywood. Founded by true Tiki lovers and outfitted by veteran carver Danny Gallardo, the Palm Springs location's vintage décor and classic cocktails have made it a Tiki staple for visitors and locals alike.

**LEFT:** A Chinese Lotus tile decanter from the Tonga Hut.

**TOP CENTER:** The Tonga Hut beacon beckons over Palm Canyon Drive.

**ABOVE:** Resin lamps, black velvet art, and flaming pupus at the Tonga Hut.

LEFT: Mojave Oasis rendering.

BELOW : The ghosts of Lake Laureen.

BELOW CENTER: The stage at Mojave Oasis.

BELOW RIGHT: Happy couple vending at Mojave Oasis.

In another example of bygone desert Polynesia being resurrected, the discovery of the Lake Loreen renderings inspired Tiki revival impresario Amy Boylan to organize the Mojave Oasis weekender at her lake property in Newberry Springs. A Tiki trailer village sprung up, an A-frame stage was erected, and Tiki wares were traded among the tropical cocktail-imbibing fans of the culture.

At the Blue Skies Village Mobile Home Park, only a few Chinese Lotus tiles remain of the Tiki Hut trailer designed by Lou Sawyer in 1960. But the Tiki spirit is carried on by new residents who created their own little South Seas hideaway in the confines of their prefab dwelling.

**LEFT:** The remnants of the Lou Sawyer-designed Tiki Hut.

**TOP ABOVE:** This home joins the other exotically themed trailers at Blue Skies Village.

**ABOVE:** A tropical haven welcomes you.

Twice a year, the Alohana Tiki Market-place at the Palm Springs Cultural Center brings together Tiki collectors of all ages seeking vintage and contemporary Polynesian Pop paraphernalia to outfit their home bars, patios, and backyards in the style. Rattan furniture, black velvet paintings, colorful aloha wear, and collectible Tiki mugs and carvings find their buyers here.

**ABOVE:** The Smokin' Tikis booth offers Tiki carvings in all shapes and sizes.

**RIGHT:** The new generation of Tiki Girls.

Modernism and Tiki style mingle in many Palm Springs homes and condominiums. The spirit of being on vacation is expressed in all its whimsical variety in these escapist interiors.

**TOP LEFT:** A Polynesian Pop pad at Palm Springs' Ocotillo Lodge condominiums.

**BOTTOM LEFT:** This casita (pool house) has been converted into a guest room.

**ABOVE:** Proud resin lamp collector Doug Thornburg in his "Afterglow Oasis."

The artist Josh Agle (aka Shag) has become the court painter of Palm Springs modernism and of the Tiki revival. His stylish tableaus of mid-century modern life display the joie de vivre of the swinging jet set that we can vicariously be part of via his paintings. There probably isn't a modernist home in Palm Springs that does not boast at least one Shag artwork.

**TOP:** Shag's *The Mammoth Martini* depicts the swinging Palm Springs jet set life.

**ABOVE LEFT:** The artist at work.

**ABOVE RIGHT:** Happy shoppers at the Shag Store and gallery.

ABOVE TOP: The annual Royal Hawaiian party during Modernism Week.

ABOVE: Shag designed his own unit at Royal Hawaiian Estates.

RIGHT: Brochure for a Royal Hawaiian architectural tour by Shag.

Of all the preservation success stories in Palm Springs, the Royal Hawaiian Estates condo complex is the most auspicious example of the joyful melding of modernism and Polynesian Pop. Every year, new residents realize their own idea of a personal Bali Hai in their units, making the yearly Modernism Week tour of the Royal Hawaiian a must-see that inspires additional design fans to join the movement.

Royal Hawaiian estates

Architectural Tour and Poolside Fashion Show

Friday February 14, 2:00 - 4:00 pm
Join us at the West Pool at 3:00 pm for a vintage fashion show, short program and refreshments

# CONCLUSION

**P**alm Springs has gone through many phases, from destination for nature lovers to resort town for pleasure seekers, from oasis for the Cahuilla Indians to ranch for city cowboys, from little Spanish village to mid-century modern mecca. Of all these incongruities, the idea of an island lifestyle in the desert seems to have been the most far-fetched, yet it seems to have fallen seamlessly into line with them, creating the fascinating heritage of Palm Springs that is still alive today and functions as a magnet for temporary visitors and permanent escapees from city life alike.

Mid-century modernism and Tiki style have experienced an exciting resurgence and Palm Springs has become a magnet for those who appreciate the architecture, design, and plain old fun of it all. The enthusiasm of the jet age went hand in hand with a curiosity for the exotic, and today people indulge once again in these innocent thrills for a brief vacation from reality. It is our hope that this book can be your guide in these flights of fancy and that the *Tiki Bird* will once again take wing to your make-believe Polynesian paradise in the desert.

# PHOTO CREDITS

# ABOUT THE AUTHORS

**SVEN KIRSTEN**, cinematographer, photographer, and author, has written five books about Tiki style, how it relates to mid-century modernism, and America's historic love of Polynesia. He also curates Tiki exhibitions, advises on new thematic restaurants, and designs Tiki mugs. Originally from Hamburg, Germany, Kirsten now makes his home in Los Angeles.

Historian and author **PETER MORUZZI** is a long-time preservationist with a passion for mid-century modern architecture and design. Born in Massachusetts and raised in Hawaii, Moruzzi graduated from the University of California at Berkeley and later attended the American Film Institute in Los Angeles. In 1999, he was founding president of the Palm Springs Modern Committee. He has authored six pictorial history books published by Gibbs Smith covering Havana, Palm Springs, Los Angeles, and Las Vegas. Moruzzi lives in Palm Springs.

SPACE FOR
PIPES AND
AIR CONDITIONING